エレメンタリー英文法

柏野健次・吉岡潤子【著】

Elementary English Grammar

開拓社

まえがき

　本書は英語の文章を読むために役に立つ最低限の情報を盛り込んだ初級向けの英文法の教科書である．対象は，大学生であるが，大学生のなかでも特に，教員になりたいと思っている人，英語の本をもっと正確に読みたいと思っている人，あるいは英会話の幅を広げたいと思っている人を念頭に置いて本書は執筆されている．

　各項目の英文法の解説は，通り一遍の解説にならないように，英語学の新知見を取り入れるなどして工夫を凝らした．そして，「なるほど，そうだったのか」という納得のいく英文法を作り上げていくことを目指した．本書の執筆に当たっては，文法用語の使用を極力おさえ，例文はやさしく，しかも読者にとって興味深いものにしようと努めた．例文の多くは自家製のデータ・ベース（最近の英米の小説・映画の台本から成る500万語のデータ・ベース）から採った．なかには，インターネットから採った例もあるが，その場合にはネイティブ・チェックを受けた．

　本書は22章から構成されていて，通常の文法項目の解説は，見開き2ページの形で17項目から構成されている．第18章では，初級向けの英文法書の範囲を超えた少し難しい文法項目が扱われている．また，第19章から第22章までは16の注意すべき構文が挙げられている．この16の構文は，これまで私（柏野）が授業で用いたPenguin Readersのなかから，授業で繰り返し説明した重要と思われる構文を取り上げたものである．巻末には，読者の便宜を考えて，簡単な文法用語の解説を付けておいた．なお，Exercisesは全章に2ページにわたって付けられている．

　本書の執筆分担は次の通りである．
　　文法項目の解説（第1章から第22章まで）　　柏野
　　文法用語の解説　　　　　　　　　　　　　　柏野
　　Exercises（第1章から第22章まで）　　　　　吉岡
　　その解答　　　　　　　　　　　　　　　　　吉岡

この教科書が出来上がるまでには，いろいろな方の手を煩わした．大阪樟蔭女子大学の Bonnie Yoneda（US）教授には Exercises およびその解答を含め全編を丹念にチェックして頂いた．本書に掲載されている英文には不自然なものはないと確信している．また同大学の Donald Kaduhr（Can.）助教授と Ann Mayeda（US）非常勤講師も協力を惜しまれなかった．さらに開拓社の山本安彦氏と川田賢氏には出版面や編集面でお世話になった．以上の方に心よりお礼申し上げる．

　本書執筆に当たり，参考にしたおもな文献は以下の通りである．
Azar, B. S.（1999）*Understanding and Using English Grammar.* Prentice Hall Regents.
Bland, S. K.（2003）*Grammar Sense 3.* OUP.
Eastwood, J.（1994）*Oxford Guide to English Grammar.* OUP.
Firsten, R. and P. Killian（1994）*Troublesome English.* Prentice Hall Regents.
Hewings, M.（1999）*Advanced Grammar in Use.* CUP.
柏野健次（1999）『テンスとアスペクトの語法』開拓社．
柏野健次・内木場努（1991）『コーパス英文法』開拓社．
Murphy, R.（2004）*English Grammar in Use.* CUP.
Swan, M.（1995）*Practical English Usage.* OUP.
Thomson, A. J. and A. V. Martinet（1986）*A Practical English Grammar.* OUP.

　終わりに，私たちは全力を尽くして本書を執筆したが，まだ不備な点もあるかと思う．利用者の方々からの率直なご意見をお聞かせ頂ければ幸いである．

　　2004 年 9 月

　　　　　　　　　　　　　　　　　　　　　　　　　　　柏野　健次
　　　　　　　　　　　　　　　　　　　　　　　　　　　吉岡　潤子

目　　次

まえがき

第 1 章	進行形	6
第 2 章	現在形と過去形	10
第 3 章	will と be going to	14
第 4 章	未来を表す現在進行形と現在形	18
第 5 章	can と may と must	22
第 6 章	could と should と would	26
第 7 章	受　動　態	30
第 8 章	話　　　法	34
第 9 章	「to ＋動詞」と -ing 形	38
第 10 章	分詞構文	42
第 11 章	比較表現	46
第 12 章	現在完了形（「完了・結果」用法と「経験」用法）	50
第 13 章	現在完了形（「継続」用法）と現在完了進行形	54
第 14 章	関係代名詞	58
第 15 章	関係代名詞 what と関係副詞	62
第 16 章	仮 定 法	66
第 17 章	I wish と as if	70
第 18 章	その他の重要事項	74
第 19 章	注意すべき構文 I	78
第 20 章	注意すべき構文 II	82
第 21 章	注意すべき構文 III	86
第 22 章	注意すべき構文 IV	90
文法用語の解説		94

第1章　進 行 形

　「be＋動詞の ing」の形式を進行形という．進行形は「しばらくの間，誰かがあることをしている」「しばらくの間，あることが続いている」という意味を表す．主語には人も人以外の物もくることができる．

(1)　I'*m making* breakfast for the kids.
(2)　"Will you marry me, Eve?"　When Eve looked at him, her eyes *were glowing*.　"Yes, Bill.　Oh, yes!"

時制別には現在進行形，過去進行形，未来進行形の3つがある．それぞれ，「... している」「... していた」「... しているだろう」という意味になる．

(3)　"I have to talk to you now."　"I can't.　I'*m washing* dishes."
(4)　I looked up at Jenny.　She *was smiling*.
(5)　I think he'*ll be waiting* for us at the airport.

ただし，進行形はいつでも上のような意味になるわけではない．動詞のなかでも行為や出来事が一瞬のうちに終わってしまうことを表す動詞，例えば① die, set, ② begin, start, get, ③ jump, knock, kick などは，進行形で用いられると，動詞の種類に応じて①「... しかけている」，②「だんだん ... してきている」，③「何度も ... している」という意味を表す．

(6)　"What's going on?"　"I have to get back to the hospital.　One of my patients *is dying*."
(7)　When we finally arrived at our camp site, the sun *was setting*.
(8)　I think he'*s* really *starting* to like her.
(9)　The sun was up and the day *was getting* warmer.
(10)　Someone *was knocking* at the door of the shop.
(11)　He *was jumping* up and down like a school kid.

　動詞のなかには進行形では使えないものもある．例えば，have（持ってい

る), know, like, see (見える), think (思う), want のような動詞は,「しばらくの間, 誰かがあることをしている」「しばらくの間, あることが続いている」という意味と矛盾するため, 進行形では用いられない.

(12) ×She *is having* dark hair and brown eyes.
(13) ×I *am knowing* him.

進行形で使えるかどうかを確かめるには, 動詞を命令文にしてみればよい. 命令文で用いられる動詞は進行形でも用いられ, 命令文で用いられない動詞は進行形でも用いられない. ただし, 物に対しては命令ができないため, このルールは主語が物の場合には当てはまらない.

(14) *Play* the piano for me.
(15) My daughter *is playing* the piano in her room.
(16) ×*Like* fish!
(17) ×I *am liking* fish.
(18) ×Blow hard! ［風に向かって］
(19) The wind *is blowing* hard.

進行形と always が一緒に用いられると,「... してばかりいる (からだめだ)」という感情を表す意味になることが多い.

(20) She *is always saying* harsh things about her brother.
(21) Tom *is always complaining* of a headache after a ride in the car.

進行形でよく使われる構文としては,「過去進行形＋when」の構文がある. この場合には,「... していたら～」のように前から訳すとよい.

(22) Betty *was having* lunch in the cafeteria *when* Jack approached the table.

EXERCISES

1 空所に適当な語句を下から1つ選んで記号で答えなさい．

1. She (   ) a detective novel, but she couldn't finish it.
   - (A) wrote
   - (B) was writing
   - (C) has written
   - (D) had written

2. Can I stop dancing soon? I (   ) to feel tired.
   - (A) will start
   - (B) am starting
   - (C) start
   - (D) starts

3. I (   ) for a securities company in New York by this time next year.
   - (A) work
   - (B) worked
   - (C) will be working
   - (D) have worked

4. She was (   ) the street when she heard someone screaming.
   - (A) cross　(B) crosses　(C) crossed　(D) crossing

2 次の下線部のうち，間違いのある箇所を1つ選んで記号で答えなさい．

1. You can <u>cook</u> <u>whatever</u> you <u>are wanting</u>, but I <u>like to</u> eat fish.
   　　　　　(A)　 (B)　　　　 (C)　　　　　 (D)

2. John <u>is resembling</u> her <u>boyfriend</u> <u>in appearance</u> <u>but not</u> in character.
   　　　(A)　　　　　(B)　　　　(C)　　　　(D)

3. I <u>had sung</u> <u>loudly</u> then and that's <u>why</u> I <u>didn't hear</u> the bell.
   　　(A)　　　(B)　　　　　　　　　(C)　　 (D)

4. I'm <u>thinking</u> <u>of</u> selling my car. Would <u>you be interested</u> <u>to buy</u> it?
   　　　(A)　　(B)　　　　　　　　　(C)　　　　　　　　(D)

3 次の英文を日本語に直しなさい．

1. "You know that I'm a teacher," she said.　Her hands were shaking.　"I tried to get work in some of the schools here, but I couldn't."　She went on.　"I don't know what to do."　She was starting to cry.

2. When we got there, he bought me a beer, and he was telling me about his girlfriend when something happened.　A pretty girl came up to our table.

4 次の日本語を英語に直しなさい．

1. 「サムはどこなの？」「あいつならメアリーと踊ってるよ．」

2. 私の犬は重い病気にかかっている．死にそうだ．

3. 誰かがドアを蹴っている．

4. おまえの車は故障（break down）ばかりしているな．

5. 通りを歩いていたら，突然，銃声（gunshot）を耳にした．

第 2 章　現在形と過去形

　現在形は，繰り返し行われること，つまり，「習慣」の意味を表すことが最も多い．always, every day などの語句とよく一緒に使われる．

(1) "Do you have a cigarette?" "I don't *smoke*."
(2) "Do you *work* here every day?" "No, I *work* here only part-time."

　また，現在形は「(いま) ... している」「(いま) ... である」という状態の意味でも用いられる．使われる動詞は is [am, are], have, know, love などである．

(3) "What do you do for a living?" "I'*m* a teacher."
(4) I *love* music.　Queen's "I Was Born To Love You" is my favorite.

　過去形は過去に起こった 1 回きりの行為や出来事を表すのに用いられることが最も多い．

(5) "What *happened* to you last night?" "I *fell* off my bike and *hit* my head."
(6) Catherine *called* a cab company on her cell phone.

　また，過去形は，現在形の場合と同じように「習慣」の意味や「(そのとき) ... していた」「(そのとき) ... であった」という状態の意味でも使われる．状態の意味では，使われる動詞は was [were], had, knew, loved などである．

(7) My husband usually *came* home at seven sharp.
(8) George was my best friend.　I *loved* him.

　過去の習慣の意味は would や used to でも表すことができる．今はそうで

はないことが強調される．話し言葉では would よりも used to がよく使われる．

(9) When I was a child, my mother *would* sing to me.
(10) Jim *used to* work here.　He took another job six months ago.
(11) In the 1980s, I *used to* work for a big company.　It was far from my home.　Every morning I *would* get up at 6:00 A.M. to get ready for work.　I *would* leave the house by 7:00 A.M.

used to の後には be など状態を表す動詞を続けることができるが，would の場合はできない．

(12) "What does your father do?"　"He *used to* be a policeman."
　　"What does he do now?"　"He's retired."
(13) ×He *would* be a policeman.
(14) There *used to* be a railway bridge across the river.
(15) ×There *would* be a railway bridge across the river.

would を使うときは，いつ，その習慣的な行為が行われていたかを示す必要がある．したがって，(16) のように言うのは不自然で (17) のように言わないといけない．ただし，used to の場合はその必要はない．

(16) ?I *would* play chess with my roommate.
(17) When I was in college, I *would* play chess with my roommate when I had time.
(18) I *used to* play chess with my roommate.
　　(cf. When I was in college, I *used to* play chess with my roommate.)

EXERCISES

1 空所に適当な語句を下から1つ選んで記号で答えなさい．

1. I (　　) golf a lot, but I don't anymore.
   - (A) play
   - (B) was playing
   - (C) would played
   - (D) used to play

2. There (　　) a statue of a lion at the gate.
   - (A) was being
   - (B) was about to be
   - (C) would be
   - (D) used to be

3. When the director got angry, he (　　) out of the room.
   - (A) will go
   - (B) would often go
   - (C) has gone
   - (D) had gone

2 次の下線部のうち，間違いのある箇所を1つ選んで記号で答えなさい．

1. Every evening I <u>am swimming</u> in <u>a</u> <u>nearby</u> river and refresh <u>myself</u>.
   　　　　　　　　　　(A)　　　　　(B)　(C)　　　　　　　　　　　(D)

2. I <u>would be</u> <u>at</u> home when the terrible earthquake shook the
   　(A)　　　(B)
   Hanshin area <u>early</u> this morning.　How <u>about</u> you?
   　　　　　　(C)　　　　　　　　　　　　(D)

3. "May I have a day off tomorrow?"　"Why?"　"My grandmother
   <u>used to twist</u> her ankle last night, so I <u>have to take</u> her to the
   　　(A)　　　　　　　　　　　　　　　(B)
   hospital.　She is eighty years old now.　My wife always <u>takes</u> care of
   　　　　　　　　　　　　　　　　　　　　　　　　　　　　　(C)
   her, but she <u>has had</u> a bad cold since last week."
   　　　　　　(D)

12

3 次の英文を日本語に直しなさい．

1. "I can't live here anymore," said John. "I don't understand this place anymore. People used to kill somebody for a stupid purpose."

2. Mike came into my office. I started my story: "My wife and I aren't together. I moved out of our apartment."
"I'm sorry to hear that," said Mike. What else could he say?
"It's okay. Early this morning, the police tried to search the apartment where I used to live. They were looking for a file that I took when I left the law office."

4 次の日本語を英語に直しなさい．

1. 私は毎日午前6時から午後3時まで働いている．

2. 剛はスマップ（SMAP）のメンバーなんだよ．［belong を使って］

3. 娘は昨日英語の試験で満点を取った．

4. 父はビートルズ（the Beatles）が大好きだった．

5. 中学時代は放課後に友達とよくサッカーをしたものだ．

第 3 章　will と be going to

　will は 1 人称（I, we）を主語にとると 2 つの意味を表す．1 つは，「... します」というようにその人の意志を表す場合で，もう 1 つは，意志とは関係なく，「時間がたてば自然にそうなる」ことを表す場合である．

(1)　"Shall I make you something before you go?"　"No, thanks. I'*ll* get a sandwich later."
(2)　Take a taxi and tell your driver to take you to Times Square.　I *will* meet you there in thirty minutes.
(3)　"How old are you?"　"I'*ll* be eighteen in January."

　2 人称（you）と 3 人称（(s)he, they, John など）を主語にとると，will は「... だろう（と私は思う）」というように話し手の意見を表す．

(4)　He *will* become president within two years.
(5)　You have a high fever.　You should get into bed and get some sleep.　By morning I'm sure you *will* be better.

　be going to には 2 つの意味がある．1 つは人を主語にとり，「... するつもり」という意味を表す場合で，もう 1 つは人か人以外のものを主語にとり，「この分だと ... しそうだ」という意味を表す場合である．このときには，何かが起こる前ぶれが示されていることが多い．

(6)　"What *are* you *going to* do?"　"I'*m going to* work for McDonald's."
(7)　I'*m going to* go and take a quick shower before we leave.
(8)　I feel terrible.　I think I'*m going to* be sick.
(9)　The sky was getting cloudy and the wind was blowing.　"I think it'*s going to* rain," said Brian to the children.

　be going to の be が過去形になると，to 以下に示されている行為が実際に

は行われなかったことを表す場合が多い．「... するつもりだったけど〜」という意味になる．

(10) I *was going to* take you to Disneyland, but because it has started to rain, I don't think we should go.

なお，be going to は話し言葉でよく用いられ，「ゴナ」と発音されて gonna と綴られる．

(11) "I'm *gonna* go get a soda.　You guys want one?"　"Sure."

will（「... します」）と be going to（「... するつもり」）を比べると，will が「その場で何かをすることに決めた」という意味を表すのに対して be going to は「前から何かをすることを決めていた」という意味を表す．

例えば，will が用いられた次の (12) の例では，主語の「私」はビルから電話があったという話を聞いて急に折り返し電話をかけることを思い立ったということが表され，一方，be going to が用いられた (13) では，主語の「私」はビルから電話があったということを前から知っていて折り返し電話をかけるつもりであったということが表される．

(12) "Bill called while you were out."　"OK.　I'*ll* call him back."
(13) "Bill called while you were out."　"Yes, I know.　I'*m going to* call him back."

したがって，次のような場面では will を使うのが適切で，be going to を用いると，話し手は前から救急箱を取りに行くつもりであったことになり，不自然な言い方となる．

(14) "Do you have a first aid kit?"　"It's in the kitchen.　I'*ll* get it."

EXERCISES

1 空所に適当な語句を下から1つ選んで記号で答えなさい.

1. If you turn right and go straight, you (　　) the station on your left.
   (A) are found　(B) found　(C) have found　(D) will find

2. "I have to go out tomorrow night, but I don't have a baby-sitter."
   "That's no problem. (　　) care of your children."
   (A) I'm about to take　　(B) I'll take
   (C) I would take　　　　(D) I took

3. "Peter is in the hospital."　"I know. (　　) him this evening."
   (A) I'm going to visit　　(B) I'll visit
   (C) I visit　　　　　　　(D) I'll have visited

2 次の下線部のうち, 間違いのある箇所を1つ選んで記号で答えなさい.

1. We are going <u>get</u> <u>married</u> <u>in</u> June <u>against</u> a famous fortune teller's
                (A)   (B)   (C)   (D)
   advice.

2. "<u>Have</u> you already read the paper <u>which</u> I turned <u>in</u> last week?"
      (A)   (B)   (C)
   "Oh, I'm sorry, I completely forgot. I'<u>m going to</u> do it now."
                                          (D)

3. "I need some money to <u>have a mechanic repair the car</u>." "OK, I'll
                           (A)
   <u>borrow</u> you some. <u>How much</u> do you need?" "Fifty dollars,
     (B)   (C)
   please. Thank you so much. I'<u>ll</u> never forget your kindness."
                                  (D)

3 次の英文を日本語に直しなさい．

1. David asked Billy what he wanted to do now. Billy suggested teasing Mary.
   "Are you going to do it?" asked David.
   Billy hesitated. "No, I'll let you do it."

2. "How's your little brother?"
   Mark looked very sad. "He's probably going to die," he said.
   "No!"
   "Yes," said Mark in a small voice. "He doesn't talk. He makes terrible noises. And he doesn't eat."

4 次の日本語の下線部1.～5.のみを英語に直しなさい．

母親「1. 何してるの？　娘を放して！」
犯人「しずかにしろ！　金を出せ！　2. 娘を傷つける気はない．」
母親「3. 主人が帰ってくるわ！　それに監視カメラがあなたの顔を ....」
犯人「4. それ以上しゃべると娘を殺すぞ！」
母親「5. こんなことをしていたら，後で後悔するわよ．」

1. _____

2. _____

3. _____

4. _____

5. _____

第4章 未来を表す現在進行形と現在形

　現在進行形は未来を表すことがある．何かの予定があって，その準備がいま着々と進んでいる場合に用いられる．心の中ではすでにその行為が始まっていると考えればよい．「... する予定です」という意味になる．

　例えば，例文 (1) では，夕食をとるレストランを予約し，彼と会う時間も決めていることなどが表される．

(1) Charles is in town, and I need his advice. I'*m having* dinner with him tonight.

(2) "What *are* you *doing* tonight?" "I'm not sure. Why?"

現在進行形は，このような「予定」の意味を表すほか，主語に1人称 (I, we) をとると，「... します」というように「決意」を表すこともある．

(3) I'*m* not *answering* any questions.

(4) "I'*m leaving* you, Ron," she said coldly. Ron was surprised. "Why?" he asked.

未来を表す現在進行形と be going to を比べると，例えば I'*m leaving* my job (next week). では「私」は仕事をやめる準備をし，会社にはすでに知らせてあることが表されるのに対して，I'*m going to* leave my job (someday). では「私」が「仕事をやめよう」と漠然と思っているだけで，会社は「私」がやめることをまだ知らないという違いがある．

　次は現在進行形と be going to が一緒に使われた例である．成人した子供と親との対話であるが，現在進行形では，話し手のきっぱりとした態度が読み取れる．

(5) "We'*re going to* get married." "Why don't you take some time to get to know each other better?" "We *are getting* married."

　現在形も未来を表すことができる．未来の出来事が確実に起こることが分

かっているときに使われる．カレンダーやスケジュール，それにプログラムや時刻表に関することに多く用いられる．

使われる動詞は begin, stop, leave, arrive, come, go, open など移動を表す動詞や開始・終了を表す動詞のことが多い．その場合，一般に tomorrow, next week などの未来を表す語句を伴う．

 (6) Tomorrow *is* Saturday. Let me take you to dinner.
 (7) My plane *leaves* for Tokyo at eight o'clock in the morning.
 (8) "She's on JAL Flight 307. It *arrives* at eight-fifteen tonight."

このように，現在形は「前もっての決定」を表すため，あらかじめ決まっているとは考えられない事柄には用いられない．

 (9) ×I *get* an A on a test tomorrow.

未来を表す現在形と進行形を比べると，現在形は「変更のできない公式の決定」を表すのに対して進行形は「変更のできる個人的な計画」を表すという違いがある．例えば，I'*m starting* work tomorrow. では「明日，仕事を始める」ことは本人によって決められた計画で，変更しようと思えば変更できるが，I *start* work tomorrow. では「明日，仕事を始める」ことは会社などによって決定された事柄で変更はできないことになる．

次は未来を表す現在形と進行形が一緒に用いられた例である．「変更のできない公式の決定」と「変更のできる個人的な計画」という観点からこの2つを比較してみよう．

 (10) "What time does the baseball game in Koshien *start*?" "At 6:00. The gates *open* at 4:00. There's a train that *leaves* Umeda station at 3:30. We'*re catching* that." "Sounds great!"

EXERCISES

1 空所に適当な語句を下から1つ選んで記号で答えなさい．

1. According to today's paper, the President (　　) for Washington at 5:00 p.m. by a presidential plane.
   (A)　leaves　(B)　will leave　(C)　is leaving　(D)　is being left

2. Naoko Takahashi (　　) the world record in the Boston Marathon tomorrow.
   (A)　breaks　(B)　broke　(C)　is breaking　(D)　will break

3. Tom (　　) the basketball club next month. His teammates want to have a goodbye party for him.
   (A)　quits
   (B)　will quit
   (C)　is quitting
   (D)　is going to quit

2 次の下線部のうち，間違いのある箇所を1つ選んで記号で答えなさい．

1. Perhaps I am leaving for Korea next month in order to interview a
   　　　　(A)　　　　　　(B)　　　　　(C)　　　　　　　(D)
   famous actor.

2. It's 8:30! What should I do? I must take the entrance exam
   　　　　　　　　(A)　　　　　　(B)
   today! It is starting at 10:00. Can you drive me to the station?
   　　　　　(C)　　　　　　　(D)

3. "What's wrong with you?" "I have a toothache." "Have you
   　　　　(A)　　　　　　　　　　　　　　　　　　　　　　(D)*
   made an appointment with a dentist?" "Yes, of course, I'll go on
   (B)　　　　　　　　　(C)　　　　　　　　　　　　　　　(D)
   Friday."

3 次の英文を日本語に直しなさい．

1. "What's your name?" Bob demanded.　The man said nothing.　"I asked you a question," Bob said.
   　"I'm not telling you anything," came the reply.

2. "I can't go back there."
   　"Why not?"
   　"The work's boring and unimportant.　I want to do something to help people.　I told you about Hillary Clinton.　Her Law Center has offered me a job.　I'm starting on Monday."

4 次の日本語の下線部 1. ～ 5. のみを英語に直しなさい．

夫 「うるさいなあ．眠れないよ．1. その番組は何時に終わるんだ？　明日は東京に出張なんだぞ．」
妻 「知らなかったわ．ごめんなさい．2. テレビを消すわ．」
夫 「2時の会議でプレゼンだから，3. 9時のひかりに乗るつもりなんだ．4. 山下君が新大阪まで車で送ってくれることになっている．」
妻 「5. それじゃ，7時に起こしますね．」

1. _____
2. _____
3. _____
4. _____
5. _____

第 5 章　can と may と must

can は，① 「... できる」，② 「... してもよい」，③ 否定文で「... のはずがない」という 3 つの意味で用いられる．③ では動詞は be のことが多い．

(1) They *can* speak different languages.
(2) *Can* you get in touch with him in San Francisco?
(3) *Can* I ask you a personal question?
(4) He is only reporting what he has heard.　He *can't* be wrong.

"can't have -ed" の形式で使われたときは，「... だったはずがない」のように ③ のタイプの意味を表す．

(5) "He was there."　"He *can't* have been there.　He was with me the whole evening after you left."

may は，① 「... してもよい」，② 「... かもしれない」という 2 つの意味で用いられる．② では動詞は be のことが多い．

(6) "Mom, if we live here, *may* I have a dog?"　"Of course you *may*."
(7) "Where's Jim?"　"He *may* be upstairs."

"may have -ed" の形式で使われたときは，「... だったかもしれない」のように ② のタイプの意味を表す．

(8) "Did you hear my phone ringing a minute ago?"　"Yes. That *may* have been Michael."

「... してもよい」の意味では，can も may も使えるが，疑問文で用いると，Can I ...? はくだけた言い方となり，May I ...? は堅苦しい言い方となる．友達に言うときには Can I ...? を使い，目上の人や丁寧に言うときには May I ...? を使う．

(9) The officer smiled and said politely, "*May I* see your license?"
(10) Hello, Frank, *can I* have a word with you?

must は，①「... しないといけない」，②「... にちがいない」という 2 つの意味で用いられる．② では動詞は be のことが多い．

(11) "I'm not hungry." "You *must* eat." Her mother's voice was sharp.
(12) She rang the doorbell several times. Tim's car was there, so she knew he *must* be at home.

"must have -ed" の形式で使われたときは，「... <u>だった</u>にちがいない」のように ② のタイプの意味を表す．

(13) "How long did you work for him?" "Almost three years." "It *must* have been a wonderful experience."

① の意味を表すには have to も使える．ただし，have to は何かの事情でそうしなければならないことを表すのに対して，must は話し手の命令でそうしなければならないことを表す．このように must は意味が強いので，それを避けるために have to のほうがよく使われる．

(14) "I'm not going to the dentist, Mom." "You *must* go, Dennis. That is an order."
(15) I guess you *have to* go back home because it's getting late.

なお，must not と don't have to は not のかかる位置が違うので，意味が異なる．must not は「... しないことが要求されている」ことから「... してはいけない」という意味になり，don't have to は「... することが要求されていない」ことから「... する必要はない」という意味になる．

(16) You *must not* lie about anything in your application form.
(17) "Are you Larry?" "Yes, sir." "You *don't have to* call me sir."

EXERCISES

1 空所に適当な語句を下から1つ選んで記号で答えなさい．

1. I've lost one of my earrings. I ( ) it somewhere.
   - (A) must drop
   - (B) may drop
   - (C) can drop
   - (D) must have dropped

2. I ( ) the movie, but I don't remember when.
   - (A) shouldn't have seen
   - (B) may have seen
   - (C) must have seen
   - (D) can't have seen

3. I couldn't go out with my friends last night because I ( ) take care of my little brother.
   - (A) had to
   - (B) must
   - (C) must have
   - (D) may have

2 次の下線部のうち，間違いのある箇所を1つ選んで記号で答えなさい．

1. She has been sick in bed all day long, so she may not be downtown.
              (A)   (B)   (C)   (D)

2. "You don't have to tell your friend who is very sick about her dog's
          (A)   (B)   (C)
   death. Will you promise?" "OK, I promise."
          (D)

3. "Mary wants to quit the company." "Why?" "Because she has never done anything except make copies for three long years."
                                                                 (A)   (B)
   "Really? She can't be bored with her job."
              (C)   (D)

3 次の英文を日本語に直しなさい．

1. I was born an idiot — but I'm more clever than people think. I can think things OK, but when I have to say them or write them down, sometimes I can't.

2. Mark took a deep breath and knocked on the door. "Come in," someone said. He stepped inside and closed the door. Three men stood there. They were not smiling.
   "You must be Mark," said one of them. "Where's your mother?"
   "Who are you?" said Mark.

4 次の日本語を英語に直しなさい．

1. 泥棒がこの窓から逃げたはずがない．この窓はあまりにも小さすぎる．

2. 彼の話は本当かもしれないし，そうでないかもしれない．

3. 交通事故のことであなたがビルに謝る（apologize）必要はない．

4. 佐藤先生，質問していいですか？　この問題が解けないんですけれど．

5. すまないが，歓迎会には出席できない．会社に戻らないといけない．

第6章　could と should と would

　could は「... できた」という意味を表すが，過去に「(何度も) ... できた」という場合に使われる．「(一度だけ) ... できた」というときには could ではなく，was/were able to や過去形を使うほうがよい．

(1)　She learned to swim before her first birthday and *could* play the piano when she was three.
(2)　×The injured man *could* walk to a phone box.
(3)　I am very pleased to tell you that I *passed* the exam.
(4)　He put his hands on the door and pushed.　He *was able to* open the door half an inch.

否定文の場合には，could not は「(一度だけ) ... できなかった」という意味で使うことができる．

(5)　I woke up at four-fifteen this morning and *couldn't* go back to sleep.

　ただし，could はいつも「... できた」という意味を表すわけではない．例えば，Could you ...? は「... してくれませんか」のように人にものを頼むときに使われる丁寧な言い方であるが，この場合には未来のことを言っていて「... できた」という意味は表していない．Can you ...? も同じような意味で使われるが，Could you ...? のほうが丁寧である．

(6)　*Could you* please e-mail me pictures of your puppies?
(7)　"I don't have any money with me.　*Can you* help me?"　"Of course."

　よく似た表現に Would/Will you ...? があるが，これらは人にものを頼むというよりも「... しなさい」と相手に指図するときにおもに使われる．普通，言われたほうは No とは言えない．

(8) "*Would you* bring me some tea, please?" "Certainly, ma'am."
　　　　　　　　　　　　　　　　　　　　　　　［主人からメイドに］

(9) 　*Will you* fasten your seat belt, please?　［機内のアナウンス］

Would/Will you ...? は場面によっては，いらだちを込めた命令の意味になることもある．

(10) 　Ray kept swinging his feet and kicking the table. "*Will you* stop that, Ray!" his mother said.

したがって，知らない人に道を聞くような場合には，would や will ではなく，could や can を使うほうがよい．

(11) 　Excuse me, but *could you* tell me the way to Macy's?

should は「... したほうがよい」という意味を表す．"should have＋-ed" では「... したほうがよかったのに（しなかった）」という意味になる．

(12) 　"I have a bad cold." "I think you *should* see a doctor."
(13) 　You *should* have married a different guy.

同じような表現に had better（「... すべきである」）がある．これは should よりも意味が強く，「そうしないと嫌なことがある」という意味で用いられる．

(14) 　You *had better* leave right now. If you don't leave I'm going to call the police.
(15) 　You'*d better* behave yourself, or I'll spank you.

したがって，(16) のように言うのは不自然となる．

(16) 　×If you go to New York, you *had better* go to the Metropolitan Museum. ［should を使う］

Exercises

1 空所に適当な語句を下から1つ選んで記号で答えなさい.

1. I'm a stranger around here. (　) the way to the nearest station?
   - (A) Could I tell you
   - (B) Could you tell me
   - (C) Should you tell me
   - (D) Would I tell you

2. My father didn't want to have a physical checkup, but we (　) persuade him.
   - (A) could
   - (B) managed
   - (C) were able to
   - (D) should have

3. "Have you told Mary it isn't your fault?" "Not yet." "You should do that." "I've tried to tell her the truth, but she won't listen to me. I (　) told her Ron lost her favorite book and that I was just looking for it with him."
   - (A) could have
   - (B) should have
   - (C) would have
   - (D) might have

2 次の下線部のうち, 間違いのある箇所を1つ選んで記号で答えなさい.

1. <u>Although</u> the fire spread <u>quickly</u>, everybody <u>could escape</u> <u>from</u> it.
   　　(A)　　　　　　　　　(B)　　　　　　　　(C)　　　　(D)

2. <u>Should</u> you stop <u>making</u> so <u>much</u> noise when I'm reading *Harry*
   　(A)　　　　　(B)　　　(C)

   Potter! I can't concentrate <u>on</u> the story.
   　　　　　　　　　　　　　(D)

3. It <u>might</u> rain <u>today</u>. You'<u>d better to take</u> an umbrella <u>with</u> you.
   　　(A)　　　(B)　　　　(C)　　　　　　　　(D)

3 次の英文を日本語に直しなさい.

1. She was wearing a wonderful dress and looked very beautiful. Freddy couldn't take his eyes off her.　He was immediately, hopelessly in love with her.

2. Kimble dove into the river.　He went under, down into the cold and dark water.　He fought the water, and at last he came up to the top. He tried to get hold of a tree that was on the river, but he couldn't. After a long time the flow of the river became slower and Kimble was able to get out.

4 次の日本語を英語に直しなさい.

1. この問題はとても難しかったけど，やっと解けた．

2. 静かに私の話を聞きなさい！［Will you ～ ! を用いて］

3. 彼女はカンカンよ．謝ったほうがいいよ．

4. 気分が悪い．チョコレートを食べ過ぎなければよかった．

5. 今すぐ金をよこすんだ，じゃないと息子を殺すぞ．

第7章　受　動　態

まず，次の2つの文を比較してみよう．

(1)　The secretary *typed* the report.
(2)　The report *was typed* (by the secretary).

(1)の形式を能動態，(2)の「is/was（など）+ -ed」の形式を受動態という．行為を行う人か物（上の例では the secretary）が主語のときには能動態（typed）が用いられ，主語の位置に，行為が向けられている人や物（上の例では the report）がきているときには，受動態（was typed）が用いられる．

どちらもほぼ同じ意味であるが，情報（information）の観点からは使い方が異なる．一般に，文は旧情報（聞き手がすでに知っている事柄で，代名詞や the がその目印となる）から始め，文末に新情報（聞き手がまだ知らない事柄で，a がその目印）を置くというルールがある．

(3)　Jim's secretary was talking to *a* customer on the phone. *The* customer wanted a BMW and he wanted it that day.

受動態の場合もこのルールが当てはまり，受動態の主語には通例，旧情報を表すものがくる．つまり，(2)では，この文の前に，「あのレポートはどうなったのか」というような文があると考えられ，そのため the report が旧情報となって文の主語に選ばれ，その結果，受動態が用いられている．

同様に，次の例文(4)は小説からの引用であるが，the door は読者には旧情報であるから，それを主語にして受動態の形式で次の文が始められ，話の流れをスムーズにしている．

(4)　He stood in front of the apartment for a long time, then knocked on the door.　It *was opened* by an elderly woman.

「by + 人か物（動作主と呼ばれる）」は，それが重要な新情報のときに限って示される．

(5) He *was awakened* by a telephone call informing him that Martin Luther King was dead.

次のような場合には「by＋動作主」は何の情報も付加していないため通例，省略される．

(6) The man *was arrested* (by the police).
(7) "Hamlet" *was written* in 1601 (by Shakespeare).

動詞によっては受動態を2種類，作ることができる．代表的な動詞は give, show, send, teach, tell である．この場合も主語には旧情報が選ばれる．

(8) The nurse *gives* the patient a sleeping pill.
(9) A sleeping pill *is given* to the patient.
(10) The patient *is given* a sleeping pill.

(9) では the patient の前の to は通例，省略されない．また，(9) と (10) を比べた場合，人を主語にした (10) のほうがよく用いられる．特に，(10) では主語には the を伴った旧情報の名詞がきていることに注意．

動詞によっては，surprise や excite のように，by のほかに他の前置詞をとるものもある．その場合には，-ed は形容詞に近づいている．

(11) The lawyers *were surprised* by the news.
(12) He *was surprised* at her response.
(13) Many young girls *are* not *excited* by competitive sports but prefer dance, aerobics and gym-style workouts.
(14) They *were excited* about his discoveries in genetic engineering.

[genetic engineering:「遺伝子工学」]

EXERCISES

1 空所に適当な語句を下から1つ選んで記号で答えなさい．

1. The secret document (　　) three months ago.
   (A) steal　　(B) steals　　(C) stole　　(D) was stolen
2. She is not interested (　　) classical music.
   (A) at　　(B) in　　(C) to　　(D) with
3. I'm very satisfied (　　) my nice husband.
   (A) with　　(B) for　　(C) of　　(D) to

2 次の下線部のうち，間違いのある箇所を1つ選んで記号で答えなさい．

1. The temperature <u>in</u> the refrigerator <u>should kept</u> low <u>so</u> that the food
          (A)   (B)   (C)
   there does not go <u>bad</u>.
                      (D)

2. A bunch <u>of</u> roses was <u>given</u> <u>for</u> Sarah <u>for</u> her birthday.
            (A)   (B)   (C)   (D)

3. Yesterday evening a man <u>on</u> a bicycle said <u>to</u> an old woman on her
                              (A)   (B)
   way home from a bank, "Where is the post office?" The moment
   she started to explain, he escaped <u>with</u> her bag. After a while the
                                       (C)
   *snatcher <u>caught</u> by two brave boys jogging along the street.
              (D)

   [*snatcher:「ひったくり」]

3 次の英文を日本語に直しなさい．

1. Tom wanted to explain how the government could protect Mark and his family if he gave evidence against the Mafia.
   "It's called the witness protection programme," said Tom.

2. One of the people of the Press asked, "How long will we be allowed to see the President?"
   "Ten minutes," said Ms. Mitchell.

3. On Thursday morning, Jake was reading a newspaper. He was interrupted by his secretary, Mary, who came and stood in front of the big desk.

4 次の日本語を英語に直しなさい．

1. 生徒たちはそのコンサートにとてもわくわくしている．

   ---

2. 彼らはそのランナーの新記録に驚いた．

   ---

3. 私がアメリカ留学中は，小さな娘はおばに面倒をみてもらっていた．

   ---

4. 彼女は手話（sign language）をサリバン先生（Miss Sullivan）に教わった．

   ---

5. このオリーブオイルはスペインから輸入（import）された．

第8章　話　法

　話法には人の言った言葉や考えをそのまま繰り返す直接話法と，人の言った言葉や考えを自分の言葉に直して伝える間接話法がある．
　直接話法では引用符（"..."）が用いられるが，この引用符の外にくる動詞のことを伝達動詞という．伝達動詞には，実際に口に出して言うことを表す say, tell, ask タイプの動詞と口には出さず頭の中で考えていることを表す think タイプの動詞がある．say, tell, ask タイプのほうが普通．

(1) "You look tired," Robert said.
(2) （Someone is knocking on the door.） "It must be Linda," he thought.

　間接話法では引用符は使わない．直接話法を間接話法に転換するときには，引用符のなかの文の種類に応じて，次の4点に注意する必要がある．① 伝達動詞を変える．② 引用符のなかの動詞の時制を変える．③ 引用符のなかの文の語順を変える．④ 代名詞を変える．
　引用符のなかが普通の語順の文の場合，伝達動詞が say のときはそのまま say を使い，「say to＋人」のときは tell に変える．接続詞には that が使われるが，省略されることが多い．代名詞と動詞の時制の変化に注意．

(3) "I'm sorry to bother you," she *said* to Morris.
　→ She told Morris (that) she was sorry to bother him.

引用符のなかが yes, no で答えられる疑問文の場合は，伝達動詞が ask であれば，そのままにし，say であれば ask に変える．語順は普通の文の語順となり，接続詞には if (... かどうか) が使われる．

(4) "Can I ask a question?" Bill said.
　→ Bill asked if he could ask a question.

引用符のなかが wh で始まる疑問文（how を含む）の場合も大体これと同じ

だが，wh で始まる語がそのまま接続詞として使われる．

(5) "When are you coming back?" she asked Ray.
→ She asked Ray when he was coming back.

引用符のなかが命令文の場合は，伝達動詞は tell が使われ，命令の内容は "(not) to ..." で表される．その場合，"tell＋人＋(not) to ..." の構文をとる．

(6) "Do your homework, Tim," his mother said.
→ Tim's mother told him to do his homework.
(7) When the phone rang, I said to him, "Don't answer."
→ When the phone rang, I told him not to answer.

話法には，このほか混合話法と描出話法がある．ともに直接話法と間接話法がミックスされたもので，小説の手法の1つとしてよく用いられる．

混合話法は引用符を用いず，伝達動詞は think を使う．上に示した直接話法から間接話法への転換の4つのルールは守られないことが多い．

(8) A person can't be too careful these days, Lucy thought.

描出話法とは混合話法から「主語＋thought」のなくなったものをいう．これは小説のなかの登場人物の「心のなかのつぶやき」を表し，日本語に直すときは「主語＋thought」がなくても「... だと思った」と訳す必要がある．(9)のように引用符なしにクェスチョンマークが出てくると混合話法か描出話法だと考えられる．どちらであるかは「主語＋thought」があるかどうかで決まる．

(9) It was dark and the rain was falling heavily. Don drove fast. There was thick forest on both sides of the road. *Where was the harbor?* After five minutes, Don stopped and jumped out of the jeep. He ran in the pouring rain. *Where was the harbor?* As Don ran forward, he heard a bird cry in the distance. *Is that an owl? he thought.*

EXERCISES

1 空所に適当な語句を下から１つ選んで記号で答えなさい．

1. My mother (　　) to break up with him.
   - (A)　said me
   - (B)　said to me
   - (C)　told me
   - (D)　told to me

2. The policeman asked me (　　) I had seen the man.
   - (A) that　　(B) what　　(C) if　　(D) and

3. What are you doing here, in New York?　Your wife said you (　　) in Chicago.
   - (A)　to be　　(B)　are　　(C)　was　　(D)　were

2 次の下線部のうち，間違いのある箇所を１つ選んで記号で答えなさい．

1. I couldn't move the piano <u>alone</u> yesterday, so I told my son <u>give</u> me
   　　　　　　　　　　　　　　(A)　　　　　　　　　　　　　　　(B)
   a hand.　He said <u>to me</u>, "I can't.　I have a lot of things <u>to do</u> today."
   　　　　　　　　(C)　　　　　　　　　　　　　　　　　　　(D)

2. "I'd like <u>to</u> thank the person <u>who</u> saved Susan."　"He left there
   　　　　　(A)　　　　　　　　　　(B)
   without <u>giving</u> his name.　He told us that <u>I</u> had done what he had
   　　　　(C)　　　　　　　　　　　　　　　(D)
   needed to do."

3. Tom told the doctor <u>to not</u> <u>keep</u> his wife alive <u>with</u> *life support <u>any</u>
   　　　　　　　　　　(A)　　(B)　　　　　　　　　(C)
   <u>more</u>.　　　　　　　　　　　　　［*life support:「生命維持装置」］
   (D)

3 次の英文を日本語に直しなさい．

1. I saw that the coach was watching me. He had a strange look on his face, and he came and told me to put on my football suit.

2. After lunch, Jake visited his client in Tom's office. He told her the trial was going to start on July 22.
   "That's two months away! Why so long?"

3. "Did he tell you what my business is?"
   "No," replied Sue. "Only that you needed a gun, and that you would pay for it in cash."

4 次の日本語を英語に直しなさい．1. と 2. と 5. は直接話法で，3. と 4. は間接話法で答えなさい．

1. 「おまえは危険はないと言ったぞ！」と彼は叫んだ（scream）．

2. 彼女は私に「Dr. Leech はこれまでに何冊の本を書いたのか」と尋ねた．

3. 先生は私に自分の夢をあきらめるなと言った．

4. その記者（reporter）は私に阪神（the Tigers）ファンなのかと尋ねた．

5. 彼は「毎朝 2 キロ歩いて公園まで行く」と言った．

第9章 「to＋動詞」と -ing 形

「to＋動詞」は「... すること」「... すべき」「... ために」「... して」の４つの意味を表す．

(1) It was raining harder by then, and it was difficult *to find* a taxi.
(2) Would you like me to make you something *to eat*?
(3) She went down *to answer* the door.
(4) Victoria was glad *to be* back in Venice with Bill.

-ing 形はこのうち「... すること」という意味で用いられる．

(5) *Talking* with a lawyer is like *talking* to your doctor. What they say is private.

「to＋動詞」と -ing 形はともに「... すること」という意味を表すが，「to＋動詞」が現実と違うこと（「非現実性」と呼ばれる）や未来のことを言うときに用いられるのに対して -ing 形は現実に合っていること（「現実性」と呼ばれる）や現在・過去のことを言うときに用いられる．

例えば，It's nice *to be* young. は若いときのことを頭の中で考えている年配の人の言葉であり，It's nice *being* young. は実際に若い人の言葉である．また，My dream is *to become* a singer. と My hobby is *reading* books. を比べると夢はこれから先の未来のことなので「to＋動詞」が適しており，趣味は現在，行っていることなので -ing 形が適している．

動詞のなかにはすぐ後に，①「to＋動詞」をだけをとるもの（want, hope），② -ing 形だけをとるもの（stop, finish, enjoy），③ 両方ともとるもの（like, begin, start, forget, remember）がある．

① の動詞は希望を表す動詞で，希望というのはこれから先の未来のことだから「to＋動詞」のもつ意味とうまくマッチする．

(6) I *want to* marry you. I *want to* live with you.

②の動詞（stop, finish, enjoy）が -ing 形をとるのは，現実に行っていることしか楽しめないし，また終えたりもやめたりもできないからである．

(7) I've *enjoyed talking* to you.
(8) She *finished packing* her own things.

③の動詞のうち like, start, begin は，-ing 形が後にくると現実性を表し，「to＋動詞」が後にくると非現実性を表すと言われる．ただし，どちらを使ってもあまり意味の違いはないことが多い．

(9) I *like walking* in the rain.
　　(cf. I *like to* walk in the rain.)
(10) I *like to* do things for people.
　　(cf. I *like doing* things for people.)
(11) Do you know when I *started smoking*?
(12) He *started to* say something, then stopped. "It's not important."

ところが，forget と remember はどちらをとるかによって意味が異なる．「to＋動詞」をとると，それぞれ未来のことを表し，forget では「これから...するのを忘れない」（否定文で使う）という意味になり，remember では「これから...するのを覚えている」という意味になる．一方，-ing 形をとると，それぞれ過去のことを表し，forget では「...したのを忘れない」（否定文で使う）という意味になり，remember では「...したのを覚えている」という意味になる．

(13) ［食事を始める前に］ Don't *forget to* say your prayers.
(14) *Remember to* wear your warm clothes. It's cold in Australia this time of year.
(15) I'll never *forget going* to a Lakers/Bulls game in NY two years ago.
(16) I *remember meeting* Madonna backstage somewhere.

EXERCISES

1 空所に適当な語句を下から1つ選んで記号で答えなさい．

1. I'm Linda. Nice (　) you, Richard.
   (A) meet　(B) met　(C) to meet　(D) meeting
2. I promise (　) you back.
   (A) pay　(B) paid　(C) to pay　(D) paying
3. Natsuko Toda says, "Translating by myself is so tough, but I really enjoy (　) friends with a lot of movie actors through my job."
   (A) make　(B) made　(C) to make　(D) making

2 次の下線部のうち，間違いのある箇所を1つ選んで記号で答えなさい．

1. "Mike, I'm listening to Prof. Brown. Please don't talk to me." "I can't understand what he is saying, Tom. His class is boring. How
   　　　　　　　　　　　　　　　　　　　　　　　　(A)　　　　　　　　　(B)
   about playing tennis after school?" "Stop to talk!"
   　　　　(C)　　　　　　　　　　　　　　　(D)
2. I'll never forget to talk with you about peace over dinner last night.
   　　　　　　　　　(A)　　(B)　　　　(C)　　　(D)
3. Daniel proposed to Karen even though he knew that she would not
   　　　　　　　　(A)　　　　　　　　　　　　　　(B)
   live long. All he wanted to do is to stay with her. However, Karen
   　　　　　　　　　　　　　(C)
   decided not marrying him.
   　　　　　　(D)

3 次の英文を日本語に直しなさい．

1. Harry said to Mary, "Nice meeting you, Mary. I'll see you around."
   "Thanks, Harry. See you soon."

2. Kevin dropped his gun. He started to walk toward the police, but soon he fell to his knees.

3. "Dr. Green, do you remember being a witness in the trial in Los Angeles in December 1992?"
   "Yes, I remember that trial."

4 次の日本語を英語に直しなさい．

1. 私たちの目的は VIP に会うことだった．

2. 父は定年後に孫とカナダを訪れる計画を立てていた．

3. 秋子のおしめ（diaper）をかえるのを忘れないでよ．

4. ドアを閉めていただけないでしょうか？ ［mind を用いて］

5. 彼らは警察官の質問に答えるのを拒否した（refuse）．

第10章　分詞構文

　分詞構文とは，書き言葉，特に小説でよく用いられるもので，-ing 形や -ed 形が接続詞と主語の働きをするものをいう．例えば，次の (1) と (2) の 2 つの文を分詞構文に変えてみよう．

   (1)   *When I* looked out of the window, *I* saw a cat running across the road.
   (2)   *As I* was tired of studying English, *I* went to watch TV in the living room.

まず，接続詞の when と as を削除する．次に (1), (2) それぞれの主語の I は，コンマの後の主語の I と同じなので，これも削る．さらに，動詞の looked と was を元の形の look と be に変えて ing を付ける．すると (3) と (4) の文が完成する．

   (3)   *Looking* out of the window, I saw a cat running across the road.
   (4)   *Being* tired of studying English, I went to watch TV in the living room.　［この being は省略できる］

　分詞構文の表す意味は，①「... すると」(after)「... するときに」(when)，②「... なので」(as, since, because)，③「... して」「... しながら」(普通，接続詞で置き換えられないが，and で書き換えられることもある) の 3 つである．現れる位置は文頭か文末のことが多い．

   (5)   *Walking* down Fifth Avenue one morning, Kay saw Tom Cruise.
   (6)   *Knowing* that I was going out that evening, I did not put my car in the garage.
   (7)   "I see," Linda said, *nodding* her head.
   (8)   "I've employed a lawyer." "A lawyer?" said Frank, *surprised*.
   (9)   There were a lot of small boxes on the table. *Curious*, she

picked one up and looked at it.
(10) *A bachelor*, Davis often invited young Parker to join him for dinner at his home.

〔(8), (9), (10) はすべて being を補って考えればよい〕

(6) の know のように，普通，進行形では用いられない動詞も分詞構文では使うことができる．その場合には ② の「... なので」という意味を表す．

(11) *Being* a young girl she is naturally interested in the newest fashions.
(12) Carter panicked, *not knowing* what to do. 〔not にも注意〕

小説では，分詞構文は，このうち，③「... して」「... しながら」の意味で，文末で使われることが多い．

(13) Men and women walked among the beautiful flowers, *laughing*, *talking* and *drinking* champagne.
(14) "I love my husband," she said *looking* away from him so he couldn't see her eyes.
(15) She stood there a moment *unable* to move, *filled* with terror.

分詞構文は上で述べたように，接続詞と主語が省略されるのが普通であるが，ときに接続詞や主語が残される場合がある．主語が残されるのは，分詞構文の主語とコンマの後の主語が異なるときであるが，これは堅苦しい言い方である．

(16) *While driving* to work, she put in a call to Tom's office.
(17) She cut her finger *when cooking* dinner last night.
(18) *Nobody having* anything more to say, the meeting ended.
(19) Mike stood there silently, *his eyes fixed* on Emily.

EXERCISES

1 空所に適当な語句を下から1つ選んで記号で答えなさい．

1. (　) what to say, the man didn't say anything.
   - (A) Not known
   - (B) Not knowing
   - (C) Known not
   - (D) Knowing not

2. (　) in easy Japanese, the picture book is good for my daughter.
   - (A) To write (B) Writing (C) Wrote (D) Written

3. (　) the lake, we put up a tent for the night.
   - (A) To reach (B) Reaching (C) Reach (D) Reached

2 次の下線部のうち，間違いのある箇所を1つ選んで記号で答えなさい．

1. Helen started to open the letter from Peter with tears in her eyes. <u>In</u> his letter he said, "I need <u>to talk</u> to you. <u>What</u> I did was very
   (A)　　　　　　　　　　　　　　(B)　　　　　　　(C)
   wrong. Can you forgive me? Can you let me love you? I'll wait for you at the cafeteria until you come." After reading it, she dashed out into the rain, her head <u>protecting</u> only by her scarf.
   　　　　　　　　　　　　　　　(D)

2. <u>Persuading</u> <u>to take</u> <u>over</u> my business, my son gave <u>up</u> studying
   (A)　　　　(B)　　　(C)　　　　　　　　　　　　　(D)
   medicine in America.

3. <u>Coming</u> back to the room <u>from</u> the sightseeing, somebody knocked
   (A)　　　　　　　　　　　(B)
   <u>at</u> the door and said, "You lost your passport at a shop, <u>didn't</u> you?"
   (C)　　　　　　　　　　　　　　　　　　　　　　　　(D)

3 次の英文を日本語に直しなさい．

1. "John was born here," she said. "Maybe he wanted to die where he was born. He left a note," she added, picking up a piece of paper. "It tells his secretary what to do after his death."

2. The fireman nodded, glancing at her. She was an attractive, expensively dressed woman in her early forties. Two women were still standing next to her, and someone had brought her some bottled water. She was crying softly into a handkerchief and shaking her head, unable to believe what had happened.

4 次の日本語を英語に直しなさい．

1. 夜空を見上げると，星が輝いていた．

   ---

2. 彼は仕事で疲れていたので，いつもより早く寝た．

   ---

3. ジョージの悪口は言いたくなかったので，彼女は黙っていた．

   ---

4. 父親に叱られて，少年は泣き出した．

   ---

5. 彼は両手を振りながら「大晦日にここで会おう．」と言った．

第 11 章　比較表現

　形容詞と副詞は比較変化（〜er, 〜est）をするが，ここでは，おもに形容詞の比較表現を扱う．比較表現には以下の3つのタイプがある．

　① 　A is as 〜 as B (is)
　② 　A is 〜er than B (is)
　③ 　A is the 〜est in/of B.

　① のタイプから見ていくと，例えば，Tom is as old as Jerry (is). は，必ずしも「トムはジェリーと同じくらい年をとっている」という意味にはならない．トムとジェリーの年齢が同じくらいであることを言っているだけで，トムとジェリーがともに3歳でも80歳でも構わない．

　(1)　Happy birthday!　You are now *as* old *as* I am.

How old ...? や How tall ...? の疑問文でも同じように，相手が「年をとっている」とか「背が高い」という前提は必ずしもない．単に年齢や身長を聞いていることが多い．

　(2)　"*How old* are you, Mark?　Tell me a little about yourself."
　　　"I'm eleven."
　(3)　*How tall* is he and what does he weigh?

　① のタイプの否定は，A is not as/so 〜 as B (is) で「A は B ほど〜でない」という意味になる．

　(4)　These tapes wo*n't* be *as* clear *as* the originals.

ちなみに，I hope he's *at least* as tall as she! のように，この ① のタイプの最初の as の前に at least を付けると「彼は彼女より決して背が低くない」ことから「彼は彼女と背の高さが同じか彼女よりも背が高い」というニュアンスが生じる．

②のタイプ，例えば，Tom is taller than Jerry (is). の場合も①と同じで，必ずしも2人とも背が高いという意味にはならない．身長がトムのほうが高いと言っているだけである．したがって，この場合，トムが160センチでジェリーが150センチでも構わない．

(5) I don't believe he's interested in her romantically. Maybe because she's *taller than* he is.

②のタイプの否定は，A is not 〜er than B (is). で，訳し方は「AはBより...であるというわけではない」となる．

(6) I am only 5 feet 4 inches tall. So I'm not *taller than* she is.

③のタイプ，例えば，Tom is the brightest boy in our class/of the three. では，「トムはクラスの中で（3人のなかで）一番，頭がいい」という意味が表される．〜estの前にtheが付くことと，in（次に場所を表すものがくる）とof（次に数字かallがくる）の区別に注意．

(7) He enjoyed Switzerland. It was one of the *most beautiful* countries in the world.
(8) A wounded animal is the *most dangerous* of all.

③のタイプでよく用いられる構文には次の「エスト・エバー構文」（著者の作った用語）がある．これは〜estの後にeverがくるもので，訳すときにはeverのところにnotがなくても「これまで...しなかったほど〜」と否定に訳すと自然な日本語になる．

(9) That's the *most boring* movie I've *ever* seen.
(10) Don is one of the *finest* men I've *ever* met.

EXERCISES

1 空所に適当な語句を下から1つ選んで記号で答えなさい．

1. Bob Sappu is (　　) than I am.
   - (A)　very tall
   - (B)　much tall
   - (C)　very taller
   - (D)　much taller

2. Akebono, an ex-professional Sumo wrestler is going to fight against Bob Sappu next month.　Akebono's son believes that his father is the strongest (　　) all the K-1 fighters.
   - (A)　at
   - (B)　for
   - (C)　of
   - (D)　in

3. "Did you watch the fight between Bob Sappu and Akebono on TV?" "Of course, that is (　　) fight I've ever seen."
   - (A)　much more exciting
   - (B)　the most exciting
   - (C)　much more excited
   - (D)　the most excited

2 次の下線部のうち，間違いのある箇所を1つ選んで記号で答えなさい．

1. The evening dress <u>that</u> the actress was <u>wearing</u> at the party is the
   　　　　　　　　　　(A)　　　　　　　　　　(B)　(C)

   most expensive <u>of</u> this exclusive boutique.
   　　　　　　　(D)

2. *The Last Samurai* was <u>released</u> this year in Japan.　It is <u>one</u> of the
   　　　　　　　　　　　(A)　　　　　　　　　　　　　　　(B)

   <u>most</u> interesting <u>movie</u> in the world.
   (C)　　　　　　(D)

3. Sidney Sheldon's books are <u>much</u> <u>more</u> <u>easier</u> than Faulkner's <u>books</u>.
   　　　　　　　　　　　　　(A)　(B)　(C)　　　　　　　　　(D)

3 次の英文を日本語に直しなさい．

1. "She's a beautiful woman."
   "Yes," he said, "but not as beautiful as you."

2. When I was thirteen, I grew six inches in six months! And by the time I was sixteen, I was bigger and heavier than all the other boys in the school.

3. The rest of the night was terrible. The worst night that I've ever known. Nobody could give us any help, and the enemy soldiers were so near that we could hear them talking.

4 次の日本語を英語に直しなさい．

1. 韓国では，ポケモンはドラエモンと同じぐらい人気がある．

2. ケビン（Kevin）はあなたほどわがまま（selfish）じゃないわ．

3. ジャックは容疑者（suspect）ではない．犯人（criminal）は彼よりももっと年が上だ．

4. あなたの人生で一番大切なものは何ですか？

5. 君みたいな我慢強い（patient）人は初めて見た．

第12章 現在完了形(「完了・結果」用法と「経験」用法)

「have＋-ed」の形式を現在完了形という．これは基本的に「過去の行為や出来事が何らかの点で現在とつながりをもっている」ことを表す．次の2つの文を用いて現在完了形と過去形を比較してみよう．

(1) My son *has lost* his wallet.
(2) My son *lost* his wallet.

(1)では，「財布をなくして今は持っていない」ことが表されるが，(2)では，「財布をなくしたが，また戻ってきたかもしれない」というニュアンスがある．このように，現在完了形はその意味が現在にまで及んでいることを表すが，過去形は現在のことについては何も言っていないことに注意．

この現在完了形のもつ「現在とのつながり」という特徴から，現在完了形には，① yesterday や two years ago など明確な過去を表す語句とは用いられない，② 主語に人間がきた場合，その人は生存していなければならず，故人は主語にはなれないという2つの制限がある．

(3) ×I've *read* that book a week ago.
    (cf. I *read* the book a week ago.)
(4) ×Alexander Graham Bell *has invented* the telephone.
    (cf. Alexander Graham Bell *invented* the telephone.)

現在完了形は，現在とどのようなつながりをもつかによって，「完了・結果」「経験」「継続」の3つの用法に分かれる．

まず，「完了・結果」を表す用法では，過去の行為・出来事が現在の直前に完了したか，あるいはその結果が現在に残っている(「...して今～だ」)ことが表される．完了と結果はときに区別のしにくいこともあるが，just, already, recently, yet などを伴うと「完了」の意味を表し，これらの語を全く伴わないと「結果」の意味になることが多い．

(5) I can't come to your party tonight—I've *caught* a cold.
(6) I'm Marty Williams. I *have just moved* into the house next to you.
(7) Your table is ready. Some of your party *have already arrived*.
(8) ［サンフランシスコで］ *Have* you *ridden* a cable car *yet*?
(9) We've got a new computer in the office. I *haven't learned* how to use it *yet*.

have gone と have been の違いに注意．have gone は「... に行って今ここにいない」という「結果」の意味で，have been は「... に行ってきたところだ」という「完了」の意味になる．

(10) Jim is away on holiday. He *has gone* to Spain.
(11) Jane is back home from her holiday now. She *has been* to Italy.

次に「経験」を表す用法では，今よりも以前に少なくとも一度，ある行為がなされ，それを現在まで経験としてもっていることが表される．ever, never, before, often などの語や three times などの回数を表す表現を伴うことが多い．

(12) I've *never met* anybody like her.
(13) "*Have* you *ever been* to LA?" "No. To tell the truth, I really haven't been anywhere."
(14) The policeman held out the ring. "*Have* you *ever seen* this ring *before*?"

この場合は，have been は上の (11) とは異なり「経験」の意味になる．また，アメリカ英語では，have been だけでなく have gone も「経験」の意味で使える．

(15) "Have you ever done any diving?" "A little. I took a scuba course in college and I'*ve gone a few times* to the Caribbean."

EXERCISES

1 空所に適当な語句を下から1つ選んで記号で答えなさい．

1. "When (　) working as a teacher?" "Three years ago."
   - (A)　you started
   - (B)　you have started
   - (C)　did you start
   - (D)　have you started

2. We (　) our house by ourselves in 1992.
   - (A)　built
   - (B)　were built
   - (C)　have built
   - (D)　has built

3. "Would you like something to eat? There is a nice Italian restaurant near here." "No, thank you, I've (　) had lunch."
   - (A)　ever　(B)　just　(C)　recently　(D)　yet

2 次の下線部のうち，間違いのある箇所を1つ選んで記号で答えなさい．

1. "Where did you get your watch? I want <u>one</u> like <u>that</u>." "I <u>have</u>
   　　　　　　　　　　　　　　　　　　　　　(A)　　　(B)　　　　　(C)
   <u>bought</u> it at an antique shop <u>during</u> my stay in London."
   (D)

2. I've <u>lost</u> my paper <u>which</u> I have to hand <u>in</u> to my teacher today. I
   　　　(A)　　　　　　(B)　　　　　　　　　(C)
   spent two weeks <u>finishing</u> it. Luckily, Tom found it.
   　　　　　　　　　(D)

3. If Tom were alive, he could give <u>some</u> advice <u>to</u> the rescue team <u>for</u>
   　　　　　　　　　　　　　　　　　(A)　　　　(B)　　　　　　　　　(C)
   saving the girl. He <u>has climbed</u> that mountain so many times.
   　　　　　　　　　　(D)

3 次の英文を日本語に直しなさい．

1. "My husband and I received a threatening phone call last night, and I've just had the second one here at the office."

2. A policeman came up to the detective. "We've searched the river," he said. "There's nothing. Nobody. I'm sure Kimble is dead."

3. "Did you see the man before he shot himself?"
"No, sir."
"So you just found him dead. Have you ever seen a dead body before?"
"Only on TV."

4 次の日本語を英語に直しなさい．

1. 列車は新大阪を発車したところだ．

2. 中田は右足を骨折したので，明日の試合には出場（participate）できない．

3. こんなすてきなラブストーリーを読んだことがない．

4. リンダ（Linda）は美容院に行ってきたところだ．

5. 彼女はニューヨークには仕事で5回行ったことがある．

第13章 現在完了形(「継続」用法)と現在完了進行形

現在完了形の「継続」を表す用法は,過去のある時から始まった状態が現在にまで及んでいることを表す.そしてそれは普通,未来にまで続くという暗示がある.必ず since, for, always, How long などの語句を伴う.

(1) You and I *have known* each other for six years.
(2) "How long *have* you *been* in America?" "One year."
(3) "I *have* always *loved* you," she said honestly.
(4) Japan *has belonged* to the United Nations since 1956.

この場合,since と for の違いには注意が必要である.since は 8 o'clock, 2001 などの特定の一時点を表す語句と用いられ,for は two hours, a week などの期間を表す語句と用いられる.例えば,2004 年の段階で「結婚して 3 年である」ことを言いたい場合には,since と for を用いて次の二とおりの表現が可能である.

(5) We *have been* married *since* 2001.
　　(cf. ×We *have been* married for 2001.)
(6) We *have been* married *for* three years.
　　(cf. ×We *have been* married *since* three years.)

使われる動詞は be, know, have などのいわゆる状態を表す動詞である.動作を表す動詞の場合は,現在完了進行形(have been -ing)を用いて「継続」を表す.

(7) I *have been writing* this report since nine o'clock this morning.
(8) I have a Ph.D. in political science and I'*ve been teaching* at Harvard for five years. ［Ph.D.:「博士号」］

まれに,動作を表す動詞が現在完了形(「継続」用法)で用いられることがある.

(9) He *has played* electric guitar for four years, and his idol is Jimmy Hendrix.

(7), (8) と (9) を比べると，現在完了進行形は，(7) のように，あることを休みなく続けて行う場合にも，(8) のように，時間を置いて繰り返して行う場合にも使えるが，現在完了形の「継続」を表す用法は，(9) のように，あることを時間を置いて繰り返して行う場合にしか使えないという違いがある．したがって，「継続」の意味では，次のようには言えない．

(10) ×They *have played* golf since 8:00 A.M.
(11) ×I *have studied* English for two hours.
〔(10), (11) とも現在完了進行形を使う〕

現在完了進行形は動作が未来にまで続くことを強調するが，まれに，終わったばかりの動作についても用いられる．この場合には，since や for は特になくてもよい．

(12) I'm cold because I*'ve been swimming* for an hour.
(13) You are out of breath. *Have* you *been running*?

このほか，「継続」を表す現在完了（進行）形については，①「... 前から」の意味で since ... ago と言うのは不自然なので避けたほうがよいという点と，② want のような普通，進行形では用いられない動詞も現在完了進行形では使えるという点に注意．

(14) ×I*'ve been* in the United States *since* two years *ago*.
 (cf. I*'ve been* in the United States *for* two years.)
(15) "I*'ve been wanting* to call you," he said. "But it's been a very busy week."

EXERCISES

1 空所に適当な語句を下から1つ選んで記号で答えなさい．

1. Joe is the person I fell in love with for the first time, and I (　　) him since then.
    - (A) love
    - (B) loved
    - (C) have loved
    - (D) has been loving

2. I've been teaching science (　　) five years.
    - (A) at
    - (B) from
    - (C) for
    - (D) since

3. "I'm very hungry. I haven't eaten anything (　　) breakfast." "I can't believe it. It's almost midnight."
    - (A) at
    - (B) for
    - (C) in
    - (D) since

2 次の下線部のうち，間違いのある箇所を1つ選んで記号で答えなさい．

1. "Lisa, have you finished your homework?" "<u>Not yet</u>, Mom. I'm
   (A)
   so tired. I<u>'ve studied</u> math <u>for</u> an hour. Please let me <u>play</u> outside."
              (B)   (C)   (D)

2. "Jimmy, work <u>much</u> harder, <u>or</u> I'll fire you." "I know, sir. <u>Since</u>
                (A)   (B)   (C)
   early this morning I<u>'ve cleaned</u> the office. Without a break, sir."
                        (D)

3. "Have you finished <u>reading</u> the book I lent you <u>last year</u>?" "Not
                       (A)   (B)
   yet, I<u>'ve been reading</u> ten pages <u>so far</u>." "Only ten?"
          (C)   (D)

3 次の英文を日本語に直しなさい．

1. "Do you remember the first time we heard that song, at the club?" said Sam. "I've been playing it since then."

2. "There's something that I've wanted to say to you for a long time. I love you. I've always been in love with you. Marry me, Carol."

3. "Is that you, Ralph?"
   "Yes, my love. Of course it's me. Have you been lonely?"
   Janet came running from the bedroom in her pajamas. She threw her arms round his neck and kissed him.
   "Why are you so late?" she said. "I've been waiting."

4 次の日本語を英語に直しなさい．

1. 僕たちは10年来の親友だ．

2. ずっと君のことが好きだったんだ．僕なら君を幸せにできる．

3. 俺はプロで10年間サッカーをしてきた．

4. ルーシーはこれまで2時間ピアノを弾いている．

5. 目が赤いよ．泣いてたの？

第14章 関係代名詞

関係代名詞とは「代名詞と接続詞の働きを兼ねる語」を指す．おもな関係代名詞には who, which, that がある．まず，who を用いた次の文を考えてみよう．

(1)　I thanked the woman *who* helped me.

(1)では，who は the woman と who から後の文をつなぐ（つまり，関係づける）接続詞の働きをしていると同時に，the woman の代名詞として helped の主語としての働きも兼ねている．ここから「関係代名詞」と呼ばれる．

(2)　I thanked the woman. ＋She helped me.
　　　　　　　　　　　　　＝ who

関係代名詞の前にくる名詞は「先行詞」と呼ばれるが，先行詞が人で関係代名詞が主語の働きをするときは，(1)のように who が使われる．

2つ目に which であるが，次の(3)では which から後の文は the convenience store の説明になっていて，which は opened の主語の働きをしている（← The convenience store opened last week.）．このように，先行詞が物で関係代名詞が主語の働きをするときは which を使う．

(3)　Did you go to the convenience store *which* opened last week?

3つ目に which はまた先行詞が物で関係代名詞が目的語の働きをするときにも使われる．次の(4)では which から後の文は the car の説明をして，which は uses の目的語の働きをしている（← My mother uses the car.）．

(4)　This is the car *which* my mother uses.

なお，目的語の働きをする which は省略されるのが普通（→ This is the car Φ my mother uses.）［Φ（ファイ）は何もないという意味を表す］．

4つ目に先行詞が人で関係代名詞が目的語の働きをするときは who（以前は whom も使われた）が用いられる．次の (5) では who から後の文は the man の説明をしていて，who は marry の目的語の働きをしている（→ I am going to marry that man.）．

(5) "Who's that?" "That's the man *who* I am going to marry."

なお，目的語の働きをする who は省略されるのが普通（→ That's the man Φ I am going to marry.）．

このほか，関係代名詞には that もある．これはオールマイティーで，どういう場合にも使える．上の (1), (3), (4), (5) のどの場合にも，それぞれの関係代名詞を that で置き換えることができる．

関係代名詞は形の上で「右方埋め込み」と「中央埋め込み」に分けられる．「右方埋め込み」とは (1), (3), (4), (5) のように関係代名詞を含んだ文が右側にきていて，それで全体の文が終わっているものをいう．一方，「中央埋め込み」とはそれが中央に割って入っているものを指す．以下は「中央埋め込み」の例であるが，関係代名詞を含む文を（　）で囲むと分かりやすい．和訳をするときは，この（　）の部分から訳す．

(6) My cousin (*who/that* lives in Hokkaido) loves to ski.
(7) The TV program (*which/that/* Φ we saw last night) was very good.

関係代名詞と be (is, are, am, was, were) が省略されると -ing 形や -ed 形が直接，先行詞にかかることになる．この場合にも「右方埋め込み」のタイプと「中央埋め込み」のタイプがある．

(8) A man *wearing* a dark suit came out the door.
(9) The lodge was a four-story house *built* in the mountains.

EXERCISES

1 空所に適当な語句を下から1つ選んで記号で答えなさい．

1. The man (　) we arrested was a lawyer.
   (A) who　　(B) which　　(C) when　　(D) where
2. I cannot trust a woman (　) tells lies to her friends.
   (A) who　　(B) which　　(C) what　　(D) why
3. Put away the book (　) you were reading before you go to bed.
   (A) who　　(B) which　　(C) when　　(D) where

2 次の下線部のうち，間違いのある箇所を1つ選んで記号で答えなさい．

1. "Where is the diamond ring <u>that</u> was in this safe?" "You <u>mean</u> the
   　　　　　　　　　　　　　　(A)　　　　　　　　　　　　　　(B)
   ring <u>for which</u> Tom gave to you?　I saw Cathy <u>wearing</u> it yesterday."
   　　　(C)　　　　　　　　　　　　　　　　　　(D)

2. "<u>Which</u> movie <u>is going</u> to take the Academy Award?" "Let me <u>see</u>
   　(A)　　　　　　(B)　　　　　　　　　　　　　　　　　　　　　(C)
   …, the Lord of the Ring.　How about you?" "Of course, the movie <u>is</u>

   <u>*starring</u> Tom Cruise, the Last Samurai." ［*star:「主演させる」］
   (D)

3. I happened <u>to see</u> the man at the party <u>which</u> my mother used
   　　　　　　(A)　　　　　　　　　　　　　(B)
   <u>to love</u> <u>from</u> the bottom of her heart.
   　(C)　　(D)

3 次の英文を日本語に直しなさい．

1. "Be careful.　There's a man over there who's writing down every word you're saying.　Maybe he's a detective ...."

2. The only important thing that happened to me at the university was the football game in Miami that year.　It was an important game which Coach Bryant wanted us to win.

3. "What am I going to cook?"　I said.　"How do I cook?"
"It's easy," said one of the men.　"Just put everything that you see in the cupboard into a big pot and cook it."

4 次の日本語を英語に直しなさい．

1. ここは安藤氏が5年前に設計したレストランだ．

2. 中国語を勉強したい人なら誰でも（anyone）このクラブに参加できる．

3. 子供たちの前で踊っているあの男性は誰なの？

4. 昨日開かれた結婚式はすばらしかった．

5. 歌だけがただひとつ娘が興味を持っていたことだった．

第15章 関係代名詞 what と関係副詞

関係代名詞には what という先行詞をその中に含んだ特殊なものがある．意味は「... すること」「... するもの」で，主語の働きも目的語の働きもする．

(1) Did you hear *what* our teacher said about the exams?
(2) Why didn't you let us know *what* happened?

関係副詞には where, when, why などがあるが，関係代名詞と関係副詞はどういう「つながり」があるのだろうか．
次の (3) の文の ( ) には which と where のどちらが入るか考えてみよう．

(3) This is the town (　　) I was born.

答えは where で，which ではない．(3) の文を2つに分けると，1つは，This is the town. で，もう1つは，I was born *in* the town. となる．この in がポイントで，この in まで含めた意味を表すのが where である．which では in まで含めた意味を表すことはできない．

一般に，関係副詞と関係代名詞の間には，「関係副詞＝前置詞＋関係代名詞」という式が成り立つ．上の例では，where＝in which ということになる．
where は，先行詞に place, house, street, town, country など場所を表す語をとる．where は「前置詞＋関係代名詞」を使って in which などで置き換えることもできるが，これは堅苦しい言い方となる．

(4) This is the place *where* I hid the key.
(5) I would like to live in a country *where* there is plenty of sunshine.

先行詞は place などのときは省略できる．しかし，先行詞を残して where を省略することはできない．

(6) He put the phone down and walked over to *where* Kay was sitting.
(7) ×New York is the place I was born.

when は先行詞に time, period, moment, day, summer など時間を表す語をとる．when は「前置詞＋関係代名詞」を使って in which などで置き換えることもできるが，これも堅苦しい言い方となる．

(8) I look forward to the day *when* we leave for Singapore.
(9) Do you remember the time *when* we fell in love?

先行詞は time などのときは省略できる．また when の場合は where の場合とは異なり，先行詞を残して when を省略することもできる．(7) と (11) を比較．

(10) I remember *when* John Lennon was killed. My biggest memory was *when* John F. Kennedy was killed.
(11) That was the day I invented a time machine. I remember it clearly.

why は先行詞に reason をとる．why は「前置詞＋関係代名詞」を使って for which で置き換えることもできるが，これも堅苦しい言い方である．

(12) The reason *why* I can't go to the party is that I don't have time.
(13) I didn't get a pay raise, but this wasn't the reason *why* I left my part-time job.

why の場合は先行詞か why のどちらかを省略するのが普通．

(14) The *reason* I'm calling you is to invite you to lunch.
(15) Do you know *why* I didn't use my credit card?

よく使われる表現に，"That's why ..." がある．前から「だから ...」と訳すとよい．

EXERCISES

1 空所に適当な語句を下から1つ選んで記号で答えなさい．

1. Please tell me about the church (　　) you held your wedding ceremony.
   (A) what　(B) when　(C) where　(D) why
2. I'll never forget the day (　　) my daughter was born.
   (A) what　(B) when　(C) where　(D) why
3. I don't know the reason (　　) she refused my proposal.
   (A) what　(B) when　(C) where　(D) why

2 次の下線部のうち，間違いのある箇所を1つ選んで記号で答えなさい．

1. Hi! This is Stevie <u>speaking</u>. I've been in the hospital <u>since</u> last
   　　　　　　　　　　　　(A)　　　　　　　　　　　　　　　　　(B)
   Friday <u>when</u> Mary works as a doctor. I'd like to put <u>off</u> my concert
   　　　　(C)　　　　　　　　　　　　　　　　　　　　　　　(D)
   till next Thursday.

2. I was surprised <u>at</u> your message. <u>I'll</u> go and see you tonight.
   　　　　　　　　　(A)　　　　　　　　　(B)
   You're just tired because <u>of</u> the tight schedule. <u>That</u> you need is to
   　　　　　　　　　　　　　(C)　　　　　　　　　　　　　(D)
   take a rest.

3. "Let me know <u>why</u> you didn't do <u>what</u> you should have done?"
   　　　　　　　　(A)　　　　　　　　　(B)
   "I forgot <u>that</u> yesterday was the day <u>which</u> I should hand in the paper."
   　　　　　　(C)　　　　　　　　　　　　　(D)

3 次の英文を日本語に直しなさい．

1. Alice walked half a mile to where she had left her car. She met Bill there, and she told him what she had discovered.

2. It took Andy half an hour to drive to the hospital where they'd taken Mary, and when he walked into her room, he was surprised by what he saw. There was a huge bandage on her head.

3. "I don't know, kid. Your story is full of holes," said the cop. "I think you were there, smoking, in the trees, and I think you saw the whole thing. That's why your brother's in shock, isn't it? That's why you're afraid?"

4 次の日本語を英語に直しなさい．

1. 君には僕が必要なんだ．だから僕は君と別れたり（leave）はしない．

2. あなたは自分のしたことに責任を持たないといけない．

3. 寝室が3つあるような家に住みたい．[where か which を用いて]

4. そこは，昨日，事故が起きた場所だ．

5. 誰でもひとりになりたい時がある．

第16章　仮 定 法

　仮定法とは「もしも ... だったら」と if を使って想像を表す文のことである．仮定法には動詞の形に応じて次の3つのタイプがある．

　　Type 1:　If＋主語＋現在形 ..., 主語＋will/can ....
　　　　　　(If we stay in a five-star hotel, it will be very expensive.)
　　　　　　(If you have enough money, you can buy a car.)
　　Type 2:　If＋主語＋過去形 ..., 主語＋would/could ....
　　　　　　(If we stayed in a five-star hotel, it would be very expensive.)
　　　　　　(If you had enough money, you could buy a car.)
　　Type 3:　If＋主語＋had＋-ed ..., 主語＋would/could＋have＋-ed ....
　　　　　　(If I had worked harder, I would have passed my exams.)

　Type 1 は厳密には仮定法とは呼ばない．この場合，if の部分で表されるのは，これから先の未来のことか，いま現在のことである．上の例文で言うと，「私たちが5つ星のホテルに泊まる」というのは未来のことで，「あなたが十分なお金を持っている」というのは現在のことである．ともに可能性は50パーセントで，if を使って「5つ星のホテルに泊まるかもしれないし，泊まらないかもしれない」「十分なお金を持っているかもしれないし，持っていないかもしれない」ということが述べられている．

　現在のことを言うときは，使われる動詞は (2) に見られるように is [am, are], have, know など状態を表す動詞に限られる．

　　(1)　We're not home right now, but if you leave a message, we will call you back.　［留守番電話のメッセージ］
　　(2)　If you know three chords, you can play almost all the songs in the world.

　Type 2 にも未来のことを言う場合と現在のことを言う場合がある．未来に関しては，出来事の起こる可能性が数パーセントしかないと思えるときに

使う．左の例文では，「5つ星のホテルに泊まらないと思うけど，もし泊まったら」という気持ちが表されている．次の例も同様である．

(3) If he failed, he would lose everything.
(4) If I saw a ghost, I would try to talk to it.

このように，未来のことを言う場合には，Type 1 も Type 2 も使えるが，if の部分で示されている出来事の起こる可能性に違いがある．Type 1 では，話し手は出来事が起こるかもしれないと思っているが，Type 2 ではほとんど起こらないと思っている．次の2つの例を比較してみよう．

(5) If I win this big race, I will marry her. ［足の速い選手の言葉］
(6) If I won this big race, I would marry her. ［足の遅い選手の言葉］

Type 2 はまた if の部分で「現在の事実とは反対の仮定」を表すこともできる．左の例文では「あなたは，いま十分なお金を持っていないが，もし持っていたら」という気持ちが表されている．使われる動詞は，(主語が I, (s)he でも) were や had, knew など状態を表す動詞である．

(7) If I had a daughter, I'd want her to be like you.
(8) "Where did he go?" "I'd tell you if I knew."

Type 3 は「過去の事実とは反対の仮定」を表す．左の例文では「私は過去に一生懸命勉強しなかったが，もししていたら」ということが述べられている．

(9) If I had known about the side effects, I never would have taken this medicine.
(10) If I had told you about Jack earlier, he would have been in jail and she wouldn't have been killed.

EXERCISES

1 空所に適当な語句を下から1つ選んで記号で答えなさい．

1. Mary would answer the phone if she (　　) at home.
   (A) be　　(B) were　　(C) would be　　(D) would have been
2. Without that medicine, my father (　　) died.
   (A) would　　　　　　(B) would be
   (C) would have　　　(D) would have been
3. We are having a party next Saturday. If you (　　) come, let me know.
   (A) able　　(B) can　　(C) could have　　(D) could had

2 次の下線部のうち，間違いのある箇所を1つ選んで記号で答えなさい．

1. "Tom proposed <u>to</u> you, didn't he? Have you already <u>said</u> 'YES'?"
   　　　　　　　　(A)　　　　　　　　　　　　　　　　　　(B)
   "Not yet." "<u>Why not</u>? If I were you, I <u>will say</u> 'YES'."
   　　　　　　　(C)　　　　　　　　　　　　(D)

2. "Long time <u>no see</u>, Jane. How about <u>going</u> to the movies this
   　　　　　　　(A)　　　　　　　　　　　　(B)
   Friday?" "I'm sorry I can't. I was in hospital for a week."
   "Really? If I <u>knew</u> that, I would have gone <u>to see</u> you."
   　　　　　　　　(C)　　　　　　　　　　　　　　(D)

3. "Professor, I'm <u>afraid</u> I'm going <u>to fail</u> English this semester.
   　　　　　　　　　(A)　　　　　　　　(B)
   Please don't give me an 'F'." "It's <u>up to</u> you. If you <u>studied</u>
   　　　　　　　　　　　　　　　　　　　(C)　　　　　　　　(D)
   much harder, you will get a better grade.

3 次の英文を日本語に直しなさい．

1. "Why did you come? Because of Helen?"
   "Because of a lot of things. I fell in love with her in Paris before I knew that she was your wife. I'm still in love with her. If I didn't love her, I wouldn't be here."

2. "I've been thinking about our future," he said. Liz's heart sank. He was going to propose. If he had done it yesterday, she would have accepted the proposal. But today she could hardly think about it. He took her hand. "I love you," he said.

4 次の日本語を英語に直しなさい．

1. もっと運動 (exercise) すれば，減量 (lose) できますよ．

   ---

2. 私だったら，そのTシャツは買わないわ．

   ---

3. 雨がやめば梅田に出かけられるのに．

   ---

4. 俊介が出場 (participate) すれば，試合に勝てるのに．

   ---

5. お父さんがお金をくれていたら，あのバイク (motorbike) が買えたのに．

第 17 章　I wish と as if

I wish 構文は「... であればいいのに」という意味を表すが，後にくる動詞の形に応じて次の3つのタイプに分かれる．

Type 1:　I wish＋主語＋過去形 ....　（I wish I were a bit taller.）
Type 2:　I wish＋主語＋had＋-ed ....　（I wish I hadn't eaten so much.）
Type 3:　I wish＋主語＋would/could ....
　　　　（I wish our teacher would give us an A.）

Type 1 は現在の事実とは反対のことを願うもので，上の例文は「（実際は背が低いが）もう少し背が高かったらいいのに」という意味である．使われる動詞は，were や knew, had など状態を表す動詞のことが多い．

(1)　I wish tomorrow were a holiday.
(2)　I wish we had stricter drug laws in the United States.

Type 2 は過去の事実とは反対のことを願うもので，上の例文は「（食べ過ぎたけど）そんなにたくさん食べなければよかった」という意味である．

(3)　This book is great.　I wish I had read it earlier.
(4)　I wish my family hadn't moved when I was young.

Type 3 は未来に関するもので，実現の見込みの薄い願望を表す．上の例文は「先生が優をくれたらいいのに」という意味である．この場合，話し手は現在の状況に不満を持ち，いらだちを込めて言っている．

(5)　I wish people would stop talking on their cell phones on the train.
(6)　I miss you so much.　I wish you would come back.

Type 3 では could も用いられる．できそうにないことを「できたらいい」と願う気持ちが表される．これには不満やいらだちの感情は含まれない．

(7) I wish I could tell you where Linda is, but I don't know myself.

as if は「まるで ... のように」という意味を表す．as though とも言うが，as if のほうが普通．後にくる動詞の形に応じて次の2つのタイプがある．

Type 1:　as if＋主語＋過去形 ....
　　　　（He treats me as if I were his son.）
Type 2:　as if＋主語＋had＋-ed ....
　　　　（He went on talking as if nothing had happened.）

Type 1 は現在の事実とは違うことを仮定するもので，上の例文は「まるで自分の息子のように扱う」という意味である．使われる動詞は，were や knew, had など状態を表す動詞のことが多い．

(8) He gave her a hug as if they were old friends.
(9) Frank tried to pass the table without being noticed. He failed. George, as if he had eyes in the back of his head, grabbed Frank's jacket and held him fast.

Type 1 の場合，as if の後に過去形ではなく，現在形が使われることもある．現在形のほうがくだけた言い方と考えておけばよい．

(10) ［家に帰って来ない主人に対して］
I feel as if you're a visitor instead of my husband.

Type 2 は過去の事実とは違うことを仮定するもので，上の例文は「何も起こらなかったように話を続けた」という意味である．

(11) The house was a mess. It looked as if a bomb had dropped on it.
(12) Two people were staring at her as if they had never seen her before.

EXERCISES

1 空所に適当な語句を下から1つ選んで記号で答えなさい．

1. I wish I (　　) a brother.
   (A) have　　(B) had　　(C) can have　　(D) could have

2. I don't feel well after eating that piece of chicken. I wish I (　　) it.
   (A) ate　　　　　　　(B) didn't eat
   (C) had eaten　　　　(D) hadn't eaten

3. "The man must be a famous actor." "No. He is only an attendant for Brad Pitt." "He always behaves as if he (　　) an actor."
   (A) is being　　　　(B) were
   (C) has been　　　　(D) had been

2 次の下線部のうち，間違いのある箇所を1つ選んで記号で答えなさい．

1. Helen had no <u>parents</u>. That's <u>why</u> she treated me as if I <u>were</u> her
   　　　　　　　　(A)　　　　　　　(B)　　　　　　　　　　　　(C)
   own mother. I wish her mother <u>had been</u> alive.
   　　　　　　　　　　　　　　　　(D)

2. "Congratulations <u>on</u> winning the prize." "I'd like <u>to</u> thank
   　　　　　　　　(A)　　　　　　　　　　　　　　　　(B)
   everybody <u>for</u> supporting me. I feel <u>like</u> I were dreaming."
   　　　　　(C)　　　　　　　　　　　　(D)

3. I <u>hope</u> I could speak another language <u>besides</u> English <u>because</u> I
   　　(A)　　　　　　　　　　　　　　　　(B)　　　　　　(C)
   want to apply <u>for</u> the job.
   　　　　　　　(D)

3 次の英文を日本語に直しなさい．

1. Sam and Mike were back in the office that afternoon. Sam looked as if he had the weight of the world on his shoulders. It annoyed Mike. Sam wasn't the only cop on this investigation.
   "I want to catch the murderer too," Mike said.

2. I got home a little late that evening, and my parents were furious when I finally came in. My father was standing in the living room and my mother was on the sofa. They looked as if a family member had died.

4 次の日本語を英語に直しなさい．

1. 君が僕の息子ならいいのに．

2. 昨夜そのテレビ番組を見ればよかった．

3. 韓国語が話せたらいいのに．

4. 彼はアメリカ映画については何でも知っているかのようにうなずいていた．

5. 母はまるで我が子を失ったかのように悲しんでいる．

第18章　その他の重要事項

A. コンマを伴う関係代名詞・関係副詞

先行詞に情報を追加するときには関係代名詞（who, which）の前にコンマが置かれる．中央埋め込みの場合は，「... なのですが」という意味になり，右方埋め込みの場合は，「接続詞＋代名詞」に置き換えた意味になる．

(1) John, *who* speaks French and Italian, works as a tourist guide.
(2) Chris appeared carrying a case, *which* he placed on the counter. (= *and* he placed *it* on the counter)

コンマを伴った用法と伴わない用法を比べてみると，例えば，The children, *who* wanted to play soccer, ran to an open field. が「子供たちはみんなサッカーをしたがっていて，全員，原っぱのほうに走っていった」という意味を表すのに対して The children *who* wanted to play soccer ran to an open field. は「子供たちのうちサッカーをしたがっていた者だけが原っぱのほうに走っていった」という意味を表す．

このように，関係代名詞のコンマを伴わない用法には，「先行詞で示される人や物のうち」という意味が含まれる．したがって，この用法では，先行詞には，固有名詞のように1人しかいないものは使えない．

(3) ×Mrs. Smith *who* is a retired teacher does volunteer work at the hospital. (cf. Mrs. Smith, *who* is a retired teacher, ...)

関係副詞（where, when）の場合もコンマを伴うことがあるが，右方埋め込みでのみ用いられる．それぞれ，and there, and then で書き換えられる．

(4) I took her into my room, *where* two men were sitting on the couch.
(5) We went to Union Square on Saturday afternoon, *when* the streets were crowded with shoppers.

B. 過去完了形

「過去完了形」(had + -ed) は小説を読むときに欠かせない文法項目である．一般に小説は全体が過去形で書かれているが，その過去よりも前のことを振り返って述べるときに過去完了形が使われる．

(6) Everyone *had* already *started* eating when I arrived at the party.
(7) Karen walked to the parking lot where she *had parked* her car.

ただし，行為・出来事を起こった順に述べていくときは過去形でよい．

(8) I saw a beautiful bird in my garden. I went to my house to get my video camera. The bird flew away. I returned to the garden with the camera.
(9) I saw a beautiful bird in my garden. I went to my house to get my video camera. I returned to the garden with the camera but the bird *had* already *flown* away.

C. 時制の一致

これは直接話法を間接話法に直すときに用いられる操作で，伝達動詞が過去形の場合，引用符のなかが「現在形であれば過去形に，過去形であれば過去形のままか過去完了形に直す」というものである．

(10) Tom said, "I'*m* feeling sick."
 → Tom said he *was* feeling sick.
(11) My secretary said, "I *made* your flight reservations."
 → My secretary said she (*had*) *made* my flight reservations.

ただし，引用符のなかが現在形の場合，その内容を話し手が現在でも真実だと見なしているときには，特に過去形にする必要はない．

(12) George said he *has* a Cadillac.
 (← George said, "I *have* a Cadillac.")

EXERCISES

1 空所に適当な語句を下から1つ選んで記号で答えなさい．

1. Audrey, (　) lives next door, is an actress.
   (A) who (B) when (C) where (D) that

2. I didn't know who he was. (　) seen him before.
   (A) I've ever   (B) I've never
   (C) I'd ever   (D) I'd never

3. Daniel (　) Japan for Seoul when I got an e-mail from him. Three hours later, I found myself on JAL Flight 903 bound for Seoul. I wanted to see him and clear up some misunderstanding between us.
   (A) leaves   (B) left
   (C) has already left (D) had already left

2 次の下線部のうち，間違いのある箇所を1つ選んで記号で答えなさい．

1. I promised my daughter to come home by 8:00 yesterday, but I
   　　　　　　　　　　　(A)　　　　　　(B)
   broke my promise to her.　She has already gone to bed when I came
   　　　　　　　　(C)　　　　　　　(D)
   home.　I'm a failure as a father.　It was her birthday.

2. Last winter I visited Paris where it wasn't as cold as I had expected.
   (A)　　　　　(B)　　　　(C)　　　　　　　　(D)

3. Jane ran up the stairs with a speed that surprised Richard, that
   　　　　　　　　　　　(A)　　　　(B)　　　　　　　　　　(C)
   hurried after her shouting, "What's happened to you?"
   　　　　(D)

3 次の英文を日本語に直しなさい．

1. The court opens at 8 a.m. and closes at 5 p.m. every day except Friday, when it closes at four-thirty.

2. Hanks left the hospital that afternoon, and drove his wife to their house, where a few friends waited with a cake and small gifts.

3. She called him as she had promised. He had read about the killing of a lawyer in New Orleans, and she told him the true story. She also told him about the other killing, which had not appeared in the newspapers.

4 次の日本語を英語に直しなさい．5. は間接話法で答えなさい．

1. ケビン（Kevin）は，5か国語しゃべれるんだけど，映画監督なの．

2. 先週，スパイダーマン（*Spiderman*）を見たわ．ブラッド（Brad）が勧めてくれたの．［, which を使って］

3. シカゴ（Chicago）で2週間過ごすつもりなんだ．そこに娘が住んでいるのでね．［, where を使って］

4. 僕たちは8月29日に結婚式を挙げたんだ．その日が彼女の誕生日だったから．［, when を使って］

5. ジョンは私に日本には行ったことがないと言った．

第19章　注意すべき構文 I

> I *saw* Ann *waiting* for a bus.（アンがバスを待っているのを見かけた）
> I *heard* the front door *close*.（表のドアの閉まる音が聞こえた）

　これは「知覚動詞 (see, hear など)＋(代)名詞＋-ing/ 動詞の元の形」という形式をとるもので，知覚動詞構文と呼ばれる．-ing がきているときは，その行為の途中を見たり，聞いたりすることを表し，動詞の元の形がきているときは，その行為の終わりまで見たり，聞いたりすることを表す．したがって，訳し方は前者では「... が<u>～している</u>のを見る／聞く」，後者では「... が<u>～する</u>のを見る／聞く」となる．

(1)　I *saw* Tom *get* into his car and *drive* away.
　　　(Tom got into his car and drove away. ＋I saw this.)
(2)　As I walked past his room I *heard* him *talking* on the phone.
　　　(He was talking on the phone. ＋I heard this.)

> Can you *help* me (*to*) *find* my ring?（指輪を探すのを手伝ってくれますか）

　help を用いたこの構文は，「help＋(代)名詞＋(to)＋動詞」の形式をとり，「... が～するのを手伝う」という意味を表す．to はあってもなくてもよい．help の後には，直接，(to)＋動詞がくることもある．

(1)　Kate *helped* her mother *clean* the table.
(2)　Bankers *help* people *to start* businesses and *to employ* workers.
(3)　I must do something to *help save* our country.
(4)　She *helped to organize* the party.

> Can you *tell* me *when* the train will arrive?
> （電車がいつ来るか，教えてもらえますか）

Do you know ...? / Can you tell me ...? / Can [Do] you remember ...? / I'd like to know .... / I wonder .... などの後に who, what, where, when, why, how, which で始まる文が続くことがある．これを間接疑問文という．直接疑問文 (When will the train arrive?) とは語順が違うことと，間接疑問文のほうが直接疑問文よりも丁寧になることに注意．

(1) I'd like to *know who* Gatsby is and *what* he does.
(2) Do you *remember where* I put my glasses?

ただし，do you think の場合は，do you know の場合とは異なり，do you think が間接疑問文のなかに割って入る．

(3) How old *do you think* he is?
(cf. *Do you know* how old he is?)

> I don't know *who to* invite. （誰を招待したらよいのか分かりません）

who, what, where などの後に to＋動詞を用いることがある．意味は「... すべきか」となる．特に，how to＋動詞の場合は「... の仕方」と訳す．

(1) I forgot to show you *how to* turn on the Jacuzzi.
(= ... how you can turn on the Jacuzzi.)
(2) I don't know *what to* do, and that's why I'm here. What should I do? (= ... what I should do.)
(3) Don't forget to send him a Christmas card. I'll tell you *where to* send it. (= ... where you should send it.)

EXERCISES

1 空所に適当な語句を下から1つ選んで記号で答えなさい．

1. Ron heard some Japanese boys (　　) about the US on the street.
   (A)　to talk　　　　　　(B)　talking
   (C)　talked　　　　　　(D)　were talked
2. I overslept this morning, so my husband helped (　　) breakfast.
   (A)　me to make　　　　(B)　to me make
   (C)　me making　　　　(D)　me to making
3. Can you tell me (　　)?
   (A)　where are you going　　(B)　where are going you
   (C)　where you are going　　(D)　where you to go

2 次の下線部のうち，間違いのある箇所を1つ選んで記号で答えなさい．

1. "Thank you <u>for</u> helping me <u>repaired</u> the bike." "<u>Not at all</u>."
   　　　　　　(A)　　　　　　　　(B)　　　　　　　　(C)
   "I'm not good <u>with</u> anything mechanical."
   　　　　　　　(D)

2. "Do you remember which song <u>did</u> <u>we sing</u> at the school festival?"
   　　　　　　　　　　　　　　　(A)　　(B)
   "*We Are The Champions*?" "<u>That's right</u>." "It was so hard <u>for</u> me to
   　　　　　　　　　　　　　　　(C)　　　　　　　　　　　　　　(D)
   learn the English words by heart."

3. Brian asked me <u>to take</u> care <u>of</u> his children yesterday, but I didn't
   　　　　　　　　(A)　　　　(B)
   know how <u>treat</u> them <u>at</u> all.
   　　　　　(C)　　　　　(D)

80

3 次の英文を日本語に直しなさい．

1. At the door Kimble stopped to help some men to carry a patient into the hospital from an ambulance.

2. Gerard was talking to Paul. "Why do you think Kimble killed his wife?" he asked. "Was he angry? Did he want her money?"

3. It was late afternoon when I began to walk back to my room. Suddenly, I heard a voice shout, "Oliver!" I turned round and saw Jenny! She had a big smile on her face, and she held my hand.
"I saw you play football yesterday," she said. "You were wonderful!"

4 次の日本語を英語に直しなさい．

1. 私は少年たちが公園でバスケットボールをしているのを見かけた．

2. ジョンは娘の数学の宿題を手伝った．

3. ルーシーは何をするつもりだと思いますか？

4. なぜ彼らが会社を辞めた（quit）のか知っていますか？

5. いつ彼女に本当のことを言ったらいいのか分からない．

第20章　注意すべき構文 II

> He *looked* out of the window and *saw* the police cars driving away.
> （彼が窓から外に目をやるとパトカーが引き上げていくところが見えた）

　look はある方向に意識的に目を向けることを表し，see は目を向けた所で何かが自然に目に入ってくることを表す．何かに視線を向けてから実際にそのものが見えるのだから，用いられる順番は look → see となる．

(1)　She *looked* up and *saw* the lights in the house.　She was about seventy meters from the shore.

　look は視線を向けることしか表さないから実際に何かが見えたかどうかは不明である．したがって，次のように言うこともできる．

(2)　We stood chatting at the sink for a while.　Suddenly we heard a sound from the door.　We turned and *looked*, but *saw* nothing.

> *It took me* a lot of time *to* find a present for Dad.
> （父にプレゼントを買うのにたいへん時間がかかった）

　この構文は，「It takes＋人＋時間＋to＋動詞」の形式をとり，「... するのに〜だけ時間がかかる」という意味を表す．この場合，人の部分は「for＋人」の形にして to＋動詞の前に置くこともできるし，省略もできる．

(1)　"What happened to John?" she asked.　*It took* a second *for him to* answer.　"John was injured in a car accident."
(2)　*It took* only twenty minutes *to* get to the station.　There was not much traffic because it was Sunday.

> *There were* some children *swimming* in the river.
> （川で子供が何人か泳いでいた）

　There is/was などの後に「名詞＋-ing/-ed」がよく続く．名詞の部分には新情報（相手の知らない事柄）がくるので，名詞には a や some/much や数字などが付くことが多い．

(1) When Oliver left the party, *there was* a limousine *waiting* for him. (cf. A limousine was waiting for him.)
(2) *There were* two clerks behind the counter *taking* care of tourists. (cf. Two clerks were taking care of tourists.)
(3) *There wasn't* much time *left*.

> I *had*/*got* a barber (*to*) *cut* my hair.　（散髪屋さんに髪を刈ってもらった）

　「have＋(多くは)人＋動詞の元の形」「get＋(多くは)人＋to＋動詞」「have＋(多くは)物＋-ed」「get＋(多くは)物＋-ed」の4つは「...させる」「...してもらう」の意味を表す．お金を払って雇った人や目下の者に当然してもらえることに対しては get か have を使い，困難を伴い努力や説得をして何かをしてもらう場合には get を使うのが普通．

(1) We're going to *get* the house *painted* by professionals this time.
(2) I will *get* the carpenter *to mend* this door.
(3) Would you please take this to a shoemaker and *have* it *repaired*?
(4) "I'll *have* the nurse *give* you something for the pain." "Thanks, doctor."
(5) He finally *got* his car *fixed*.
(6) Mary did her best to *get* him *to give* up smoking.
　 (cf. ×Mary did her best to *have* him *give* up smoking.)

EXERCISES

1 空所に適当な語句を下から1つ選んで記号で答えなさい．

1. It took him three days (　　) the jigsaw puzzle.
   (A) finish　　(B) finished　　(C) to finish　　(D) finishing

2. There were three students (　　) for the test in the library.
   (A) study　　(B) studied　　(C) to study　　(D) studying

3. Someone called my name, so I turned around and (　　) a man holding a knife in his hand. I was so scared! I screamed out, "Help me!"
   (A) looked　　(B) looked at　　(C) saw　　(D) saw at

2 次の下線部のうち，間違いのある箇所を1つ選んで記号で答えなさい．

1. "Richard, wake up! It's time to leave for school!" "Mom, I had
   　　　　　　　　(A)　　　　　　　　　　　　　(B)
   only a little sleep last night. It took five hours of me to finish my
   　　　　　　　　　　　　　　　　　　　　　　　　(C)　(D)
   homework. Let me sleep just a little more, please."

2. There were a lot of fans waited for me at Kansai Airport when I
   　　　　　　　　　　　　(A)　　　　　(B)　　　　　　　　　　(C)
   got off the plane.
   　　(D)

3. Though my father was reluctant to drive a car, I finally got him
   (A)　　　　　　　　　　　(B)
   drove me to the airport. I don't know how to thank him.
   (C)　　　　　　　　　　　　　　　　　(D)

3 次の英文を日本語に直しなさい．

1. There were two girls working there. One was tall and the other was wearing glasses.

2. The baseball game was canceled because of the rain. Ichiro changed his clothes in the locker room, then had his driver take him straight from the stadium to the hospital, for he had felt a sharp pain in his back.

3. The next day the big chess tournament was held at the Beverly Hills Hotel. Jake and I got there early, and I had to play chess all day. It took me about seven minutes to win the first game, and half an hour to win the next.

4 次の日本語を英語に直しなさい．

1. 彼女の作文を添削する（correct）のに30分かかった．

   ------

2. 美術館内では10人のボディガードがダイアナ妃を警護（protect）していた．

   ------

3. 彼女の家の前に緑色の車が止まって（park）いた．［Thereで始めて］

   ------

4. 真夜中に孫娘の往診（come and see）をしてもらった．

   ------

5. 彼は秘書にスケジュールをチェックしてもらった．

第21章　注意すべき構文Ⅲ

> She was reading, *with* the television on.
> （彼女はテレビをつけたままで読書をしていた）

with A B の形式で「A を B のままにして」という意味で用いる．A には（代）名詞，B には形容詞，前置詞，-ed 形，-ing 形などがくる．ときに例文(5)のように，with は省略されてコンマになることがある．

(1) The shark swam towards the shore, *with* its eyes and mouth open.
(2) He slept in a chair *with* a hat over his face.
(3) She was sitting on her bed *with* her legs crossed.
 (cf. Her legs were crossed.)
(4) The dinosaur ran away *with* a piece of meat hanging from its mouth.　(cf. A piece of meat was hanging from its mouth.)
(5) When Tim walked into the room, Jenny stood there in a beautiful gown, a big smile on her face.

> They *sat sipping* their drinks.　（彼らは座って飲み物をすすっていた）

sit, stand, lie の後に -ing を続けて「座った［立った，横になった］ままで…している」という意味で用いる．例文(2), (3)のように動詞と -ing の間に場所を表す語句が入ることもある．この場合には分詞構文に近づく．

(1) The old man *stood looking* out of the window in silence.
(2) I *sat* there *smoking* and *reading* the magazines.
(3) Kate *lay* in bed, *thinking* about Joe.

> He *caught* her *by* the wrist.（彼は彼女の手首をつかんだ）

　この構文は接触動詞構文と呼ばれる．接触動詞とは，① たたく（hit），触る（touch），ける（kick），② つかむ（take, catch），ひっぱる（pull）など人体と何らかの接触を表す動詞を指す．① では「接触動詞＋人＋on/in＋the＋体の部分」，② では「接触動詞＋人＋by＋the＋体の部分」という形式をとる．このほか，例文 (5) のように「接触動詞＋his/her など＋体の部分」の構文も可能である．なお，kiss も接触動詞として ① に分類されることがある．

(1)　He *kicked* me *in* the stomach.
(2)　The woman *hit* him *in* the face with the newspaper.
(3)　He raised his gun to *hit* George *on* the head.
(4)　Sue reached for him and *pulled* him *by* the hand.
(5)　He *took* her hand. "Marry me, Elsa."

> There was something odd about him.
> （彼にはどことなく，おかしなところがあった）

　これは There is/was something A about/with B という構文で A には形容詞，B には人や物がくる．「どことなく ... なところがある」という日本語をこの構文を用いて英語に直すことができる．例文 (4) のように，A には形容詞ではなく，関係代名詞がくることもある．その場合には関係代名詞を含む文は後に置かれる．

(1)　There was something very special about George.
(2)　There is something funny about this.
(3)　I think there was something wrong with the fire alarm system.
(4)　There was something about her that touched him deeply.

EXERCISES

1 空所に適当な語句を下から1つ選んで記号で答えなさい．

1. He was lying on the sofa with his (　　)．
   (A) arms folded　　　(B) arms folding
   (C) fold arms　　　　(D) folding arms

2. She touched him (　　) arm and said, "Stand back from the white line."
   (A) on a　　(B) on the　　(C) by a　　(D) by the

3. There is something (　　) him that makes us happy.
   (A) about　　(B) for　　(C) of　　(D) to

2 次の下線部のうち，間違いのある箇所を1つ選んで記号で答えなさい．

1. You <u>must not</u> stand <u>by</u> your hands <u>in</u> your <u>pockets</u>.
   　　　(A)　　　　　(B)　　　　　(C)　　　(D)

2. I was surprised <u>to see</u> an elementary school boy <u>standing</u>
   　　　　　　　　　(A)　　　　　　　　　　　　　　　(B)
   <u>done</u> his math homework <u>on</u> the train.
   　(C)　　　　　　　　　　　(D)

3. I <u>lost</u> my way in the woods.　It <u>was getting</u> dark.　I was so scared!
   　　(A)　　　　　　　　　　　　(B)
   I tried <u>to contact</u> the police by cell phone, but I couldn't.　All of a
   　　　　(C)
   sudden, someone grabbed me by <u>an</u> ankle.　I almost fainted.
   　　　　　　　　　　　　　　　　(D)

3 次の英文を日本語に直しなさい．

1. Pola was lying on the bed, watching TV. It was eleven at night. She decided that she would wait until twelve but fell asleep.

2. It was going to be a sunny day; the birds were singing in the morning light, traffic was moving, most people were going to work with sunglasses on.

3. She reached out and touched Jack on the end of his nose with her index finger.

4 次の日本語を英語に直しなさい．

1. 玄関のドアに鍵をかけないで家を出て行ってはいけない．

2. ベッカム（Beckham）は歓迎会で少女の頬にキスをした．

3. 彼女はジョン・レノンのイマジンをソファーに座って歌っていた．

4. 彼にはどことなくあやしい（strange）ところがある．

5. 私のコンピューターはどこかおかしい．

第22章　注意すべき構文Ⅳ

> The *key* opened the door.　（鍵を使うとドアが開いた）

これは，無生物主語構文と呼ばれるもので，主語にきている無生物が動詞で示される行為や出来事の手段や原因となっている．そのまま日本語にすると不自然なので，無生物主語のところを「... すると」「... のために」などと工夫をして訳すとよい．よく用いられる動詞は make と take である．

(1) He called 911, and an *ambulance* took his mother to the hospital.
(2) She lay on the sofa and looked at the newspaper. The *front page* surprised her.
(3) Maria came into the room with a cup of tea. "Here. *This* will make you feel better." She looked at him. "Is everything all right?"

> He *watched as* she dried her hair.
> （彼は彼女が髪を乾かしているのをじっと見ていた）

「watch＋（人）＋as＋主語＋動詞」の形式で用いられるもので，知覚動詞構文の「watch＋人＋-ing」を用いて書き換えられる．上の例であれば，He watched her drying her hair. となる．

(1) She *watched* Don *as* he opened a bottle of champagne.
(2) He *watched as* the expression on her face became more and more serious.
(3) Jim *watched as* she poured the tea. "Would you like a cake?" "No, thanks."

> He *tried to* climb the tree, *but* failed.
> （彼は木に登ろうとしたが，失敗した）

try の後には「to＋動詞」も -ing もくるが，「to＋動詞」のほうが圧倒的によく用いられる．その場合には but が後続することが多い．何かを試みようとしたが，失敗したことが表される．

(1) He put his arm around her, *tried to* kiss her, *but* Jody moved away from him.
(2) She *tried to* scream, *but* no sound came out of her mouth. She *tried to* move, *but* she couldn't.
(3) I *tried to* get in touch with him several times, *but* he didn't return my calls.

> They *waited for* the waiter *to* set the table.
> （彼らはウエイターがテーブルの用意をするのを待った）

wait は「...を待つ」の意味で，例えば He was waiting for a bus. のように for をとるが，さらにその後に「to＋動詞」を従え，「wait for＋人・物＋to＋動詞」の形式でもよく用いられる．「人や物が...するのを待つ」という意味になる．

(1) He *waited for* the applause *to* die down.
(2) Rescue teams were *waiting for* the weather *to* become better.
(3) They *waited and waited for* him *to* turn up but he didn't.
(4) She *waited for* him *to* say that he loved her, or missed her, but he didn't.

EXERCISES

1 空所に適当な語句を下から1つ選んで記号で答えなさい．

1. This book will (　　) the importance of education.
   - (A) make you understand
   - (B) make to understand you
   - (C) make you understanding
   - (D) make you understood

2. A car (　　) to a small airfield, where a private jet was waiting for him.
   - (A) Kevin took
   - (B) took Kevin
   - (C) Kevin made
   - (D) made Kevin

3. The nurse watched as the patient (　　) to the bed.
   - (A) walk
   - (B) to walk
   - (C) walking
   - (D) walked

2 次の下線部のうち，間違いのある箇所を1つ選んで記号で答えなさい．

1. One <u>of</u> the passengers happened <u>to watch</u> the man <u>to put</u> a bomb
       (A)   (B)   (C)
   under the seat. His report <u>to</u> the pilot saved a lot of people's lives.
                                (D)

2. Carol was trying to look <u>as if</u> she <u>weren't</u> upset <u>about</u> the news, <u>and</u>
                              (A)   (B)   (C)   (D)
   she couldn't.

3. "I'm sorry <u>to have</u> kept you <u>waiting</u> so long, Mike." "<u>No</u> problem,
                (A)   (B)   (C)
   Joe." "Can we stay here a little longer? I want to wait <u>of</u> Sue to
                                                              (D)
   come out of the library so that I can give her these roses."

3 次の英文を日本語に直しなさい．

1. Reggie watched as Mark and Diane walked back to the plane. Suddenly Mark turned. "Aren't you coming, Reggie?" he asked. "No, Mark. I can't. I love you, Mark. I'll miss you."

2. She was furious with herself and with the fool who gave her directions. She turned around and tried to find her way back, but soon she was on unfamiliar roads again.

3. I saw the short man who chased me last week come up to a woman. They talked for a minute and then the short man disappeared again. They're waiting for us to leave the building.

4 次の日本語を英語に直しなさい．

1. このバスに乗れば大阪城に行けるよ．

2. この映画でトム・クルーズ（Tom Cruise）は国際的な俳優になった．
   ［make を使って］

3. カレン（Karen）は吉田兄弟が三味線を弾いているのをじっと見ていた．

4. 健太はおもちゃ屋まで歩いて行こうとしたが，道に迷ってしまった．

5. 両親は娘がアメリカから帰国するのをずっと待っている．

文法用語の解説
（用語のアイウエオ順に掲載）

[ア行]
受身
　→受動態

[カ行]
堅苦しい言い方
　知らない人や目上の人と丁寧に話をする場合に用いられる言葉のこと．例えば，以下に挙げる語は（　）内に示した語よりも堅苦しい語である．cease (stop), close (shut), complete (finish), inquire (ask), obtain (get), purchase (buy), remark (say), seek (look for)．また，I am afraid I have no information. は Sorry, I don't know. よりも堅苦しい言い方となる．

間接話法
　人の言った言葉や考えを自分の言葉に直して伝える話法で，直接話法からこの話法に転換するときには伝達動詞，時制，語順，代名詞などを変える必要がある．
　（1）　Tom said to us, "Where are you going?"
　　　→ Tom asked us where we were going.

くだけた言い方
　日常，友達と話をするときに使う言葉のこと．縮約形や省略は，くだけた言い方の特徴である．
　（1）　I think (that) he's (=he is) in love with you.

コンマを伴った関係代名詞・関係副詞
　正確には関係代名詞・関係副詞の「非制限的（あるいは非限定的）用法」という．例えば，My *cousin, who* lives in LA, calls me every weekend. は「僕のいとこはロスに住んでいるのですが，週末ごとに電話をかけてくる」という意味で，who 以下は単に my cousin についての情報を追加しているだけである．ここでは，話し手にはいとこは1人しかいないという意味になる．

コンマを伴わない関係代名詞・関係副詞
　正確には関係代名詞・関係副詞の「制限的（あるいは限定的）用法」という．例えば，My *cousin who* lives in LA calls me every weekend. は「僕のいとこのうちロスに住んでいる者が週末ごとに電話をかけてくる」という意味で，who 以下でこのいとこと他の所に住んでいるいとこが区別されていて，話し手には2人以

上のいとこがいることが暗に示されている．

[サ行]
時制
　動詞の形によって時間の関係（現在か過去）を表したもの．例えば，play であれば，play が現在時制を表し，語尾に -ed を付けた played が過去時制を表す．
　(1)　I *play* the violin every day.
　(2)　We *played* baseball in the park yesterday.
英語では動詞の形を変えることによって未来を表すことはできない．未来を表すためには will や be going to などの助けを借りないといけない．
　(3)　The band *will play* the American national anthem.

受動態
　受動態は「is/was（など）＋-ed」の形式をとる．例えば，is broken, was told などがその例である．行為が向けられている人や物に焦点を当てたい場合にこの受動態が用いられる．受身ともいう．
　(1)　Somebody built this house in 1980.
　　　→ This house *was built* in 1980.

接続詞
　簡単に言えば，and, but, although, because, when, if のような語で，文（正確には節）や語句などをつなぐのに用いられる語のこと．
　(1)　I'm sorry, *but* I'm not sure.
　(2)　She's tall *and* thin.

[タ行]
代名詞
　I, you, she, he, it のように名詞の代わりをする語のこと．
　(1)　Meg is not coming with us.　*She* is not very well.

直接話法
　話し手が時制，代名詞などを変えずに人の言った言葉や考えをそのまま引用符を用いて繰り返す話法のことである．
　(1)　"I'm tired," Jenny said.
　(2)　Tracy thought, "Oh, my God.　I'm dressed all wrong!　I should have worn the Yves Saint Laurent."

伝達動詞
　直接話法や間接話法で使われる say, tell, ask などの動詞のことで，言われた，あ

るいは考えられた内容を伝えるもの．

動作主

受動態の文では動作主とは行為を行う人または物のことで，by によって導かれる．例えば，This picture was painted *by a child*. では child が動作主となる．

動詞

動詞には動作を表すもの（arrive, break, dream, eat）と状態を表すもの（belong, have, know, like）がある．動作を表す動詞には，その動作が arrive, break のように瞬間的に終わってしまうものと dream, eat のように一定時間，続くものがある．動作を表す動詞は進行形にできるが，状態を表す動詞は進行形にはできない．瞬間的に終わってしまうことを示す動詞が進行形で用いられた場合に表す意味については p. 6 を参照．

動詞の元の形

正確には動詞の「原形」という．辞書の見出し語にあるような基本的な動詞の形のことである．多くは現在形と同じであるが，am, are, is, was, were の原形は be である．

[ナ行]

人称

人称には 1 人称，2 人称，3 人称がある．1 人称は話し手（I, we）のことで，2 人称は話し相手（you）のことである．3 人称とは話題に上っている人や物（he, she, they, it, John など）を指す．

(1)　*I* told *him* all about *you*, and *he* wanted to meet *you* very much.

能動態

能動態の動詞とは，例えば，break, studied, will come のような形をいう．能動態の動詞の主語は普通，その動詞が表す行為を行ったり，出来事を引き起こしたりする人または物である．

(1)　The angry man *broke* the vase with a hammer.
(2)　How did the accident *happen*?